Other Publications:

UNDERSTANDING COMPUTERS
YOUR HOME
THE ENCHANTED WORLD
THE KODAK LIBRARY OF CREATIVE PHOTOGRAPHY
GREAT MEALS IN MINUTES
THE CIVIL WAR
PLANET EARTH
COLLECTOR'S LIBRARY OF THE CIVIL WAR
THE EPIC OF FLIGHT
THE GOOD COOK
WORLD WAR II
THE OLD WEST

For information on and a full description of any of the Time-
Life Books series listed above, please write:
Reader Information
Time-Life Books
541 North Fairbanks Court
Chicago, Illinois 60611

This volume is part of a series offering homeowners
detailed instructions on repairs, construction
and improvements they can undertake themselves.

HOME REPAIR
AND IMPROVEMENT

LANDSCAPING

BY THE EDITORS OF
TIME-LIFE BOOKS

TIME-LIFE BOOKS
ALEXANDRIA, VIRGINIA

Time-Life Books Inc.
is a wholly owned subsidiary of
TIME INCORPORATED

Founder	Henry R. Luce 1898-1967

Editor-in-Chief	Henry Anatole Grunwald
President	J. Richard Munro
Chairman of the Board	Ralph P. Davidson
Corporate Editor	Ray Cave
Group Vice President, Books	Reginald K. Brack Jr.
Vice President, Books	George Artandi

TIME-LIFE BOOKS INC.

Editor	George Constable
Executive Editor	George Daniels
Editorial General Manager	Neal Goff
Director of Design	Louis Klein
Director of Editorial Resources	Phyllis K. Wise
Editorial Board	Dale M. Brown, Roberta Conlan, Ellen Phillips, Donia Ann Steele, Rosalind Stubenberg, Kit van Tulleken, Henry Woodhead
Director of Research and Photography	John Conrad Weiser
President	Reginald K. Brack Jr.
Executive Vice Presidents	John M. Fahey Jr., Christopher T. Linen
Senior Vice President	James L. Mercer
Vice Presidents	Stephen L. Bair, Edward Brash, Ralph J. Cuomo, Juanita T. James, Wilhelm R. Saake, Robert H. Smith, Paul R. Stewart, Leopoldo Toralballa

HOME REPAIR AND IMPROVEMENT

Editor	John Paul Porter
Deputy Editor	William Frankel
Designer	Edward Frank

Editorial Staff for Landscaping

Associate Editors	Mark M. Steele, Brooke C. Stoddard
Text Editors	Lynn R. Addison, William Worsley
Staff Writers	Kevin D. Armstrong, Patricia C. Bangs, Deborah Berger-Turnbull, Carol Jane Corner, Rachel Cox, Leon Greene, Kathleen M. Kiely, Victoria W. Monks, Kirk Y. Saunders
Copy Coordinator	Stephen G. Hyslop
Art Assistants	George Bell, Fred Holz, Lorraine D. Rivard, Peter C. Simmons
Editorial Assistant	Myrna E. Traylor
Picture Coordinator	Renée DeSandies
Special Contributors	William Doyle, Lydia Preston, David Thiemann

Editorial Operations

Copy Chief	Diane Ullius
Editorial Operations	Caroline A. Boubin (manager)
Production	Celia Beattie
Quality Control	James J. Cox (director)
Library	Louise D. Forstall

Correspondents: Elisabeth Kraemer-Singh (Bonn); Dorothy Bacon (London); Maria Vincenza Aloisi, Josephine du Brusle (Paris); Ann Natanson (Rome).

THE CONSULTANTS: Roswell W. Ard is a consulting structural engineer and a professional home inspector in northern Michigan. He has written widely on house construction.

Harris Mitchell, special consultant for Canada, has worked in the field of home repair and improvement since 1950. He writes a syndicated newspaper column, "You Wanted to Know," and is author of a number of books on home improvement.

Jane Krumbhaar, a landscape designer, operates a landscape contracting and design firm serving urban and suburban homeowners in the Washington, D.C., area.

Dr. Alex L. Shigo is Chief Scientist at the Northeastern Experiment Station, United States Forest Service, in Durham, New Hampshire. The recipient of numerous awards and the author of more than 200 technical publications, he has pioneered research on the care of trees.

George Sliker, a landscape contractor and nurseryman, owns and runs The Green Landing Nursery of Upper Marlboro, Maryland.

Colonel Charles A. H. Thomson, USA (Ret.), is co-author of *Successful Gardening*. An authority on the horticulture of both the West and East coasts of North America, he has lectured at the Smithsonian Institution, the United States National Arboretum and the Department of Agriculture.

Nancy Willis Keyes is a landscape architect who has designed parks and homeowners' properties over an area ranging from the Midwest to the East Coast.

Time-Life Books Inc. offers a wide range of fine recordings, including a *Rock 'n' Roll Era* series. For subscription information, call 1-800-621-7026 or write Time-Life Music, P.O. Box C-32068, Richmond, Virginia 23261-2068.

Library of Congress Cataloguing in Publication Data
Main entry under title:
Landscaping.
  (Home repair and improvement)
  Includes index.
  1. Landscape gardening. I. Time-Life Books. II. Series.
SB473.L3683 1983   635.9   82-19374
ISBN 0-8094-3514-4
ISBN 0-8094-3515-2 (lib. bdg.)

Contents

Organizing the Outdoors

Analyzing the earth. In a soil test, a bit of garden earth at the bottom of a test tube is exposed to a chemical that will help disclose its composition. Each such chemical (available in test kits at garden-supply stores) changes color when it mixes with the soil. Color charts that come with the kits are matched with the colored chemicals to determine the soil's concentrations of such nutrient elements as nitrogen, potassium (indicated in the form of potash, a potassium compound) and phosphorus.

There was a time when the word "landscaping" evoked images of immaculate lawns and elegant gardens, designed by landscape architects and meticulously maintained by platoons of gardeners and nurserymen. But times have changed. Today, many of the landscaping principles and techniques that have been used for centuries to beautify parks and estates are converting suburban yards and tiny townhouse gardens into pleasant, functional environments—without professional help and often at surprisingly low cost.

Landscaping is simply the organization of outdoor space to provide much the same sorts of amenities—privacy, comfort, beauty and ease of maintenance—that are built into the indoor space of a home. Just as the interior of a house can be modified by basic woodworking, plumbing and wiring skills, so the land around it can be reshaped by the techniques delineated in this volume: clearing and leveling earth; planting and nurturing lawns, shrubs, trees, vines and flowers; and assembling or building such structures as garden pools, rock gardens and trellises or arbors. It is possible, in fact, to plan a yard as a kind of oversized family room, with walls of hedges and fences; ceilings of sky, shade trees and arbors; and floors of grasses and ground covers. A comprehensive landscaping plan includes all of these elements, along with such decorative additions as flower beds and man-made ornaments ranging from a modest fountain to a terraced swimming pool.

A good plan *(pages 16-21)* not only meets individual tastes and requirements, but takes the uniqueness of the land itself into consideration. No two pieces of property are exactly the same, even when their dimensions and the houses built upon them are identical. A yard may be overgrown or barren, level or uneven, sunlit or shaded, moist or dry. The site may originally have been an ancient swamp, forest or farmland, with soil enriched by natural or chemical fertilizers—or it may be a rocky outcrop filled with rubble in which only the hardiest plants will grow. It is as important to know the limitations of your land as it is to know its potential. Simple tests *(pages 32-34)* tell whether the soil is sandy, clayey or loamy, and kits like the one shown opposite reveal soil chemistry—the presence of basic nutrients, and the degree of acidity or alkalinity.

Fortunately, most deficiencies are correctible. Armed with the proper tools *(pages 8-11)*, even a novice can remove rocks and stumps, level ridges and depressions, grade slopes, dig drainage ditches, erect retaining walls, and enrich the soil or alter its chemistry to encourage plant growth. With these preparations completed, a landscaping plan can be made a reality, transforming your speck of the earth's surface into an enclosure of singular beauty and utility.

A Landscaper's Tool Kit

Like every other craft, landscaping calls for specialized tools. Some, such as those shown here, are in frequent use; others, such as those on pages 10-11, are needed less often. A beginning landscaper should consider buying all or most of the tools in this first group (they are listed below according to function).

□ HAND GARDENING. Small tools for individual plants and flower beds are generally sold as a four-piece set—cultivator, trowel, hand fork and weeding fork.

□ PRUNING AND TRIMMING. A pair of pruning shears can sever branches up to ½ inch thick; lopping shears can slice branches up to 1 inch thick; still larger limbs are trimmed with a curved, coarse-toothed pruning saw. High branches can be cut with pole shears, which have a pulley-operated cutter and a removable saw blade. Ragged shrubs should be trimmed with scissor-like hedge shears.

□ DIGGING. A pointed, short-handled spade is ideal for turning soil; the long-handled spade is used for excavations more than a foot deep. A square-nosed, short-handled spade knifes through tree roots and digs neat trenches. A spading fork turns compost and moist soil, which stick to spades.

□ TILLING. The most versatile tool for cultivating the soil is an old-fashioned hoe; a bow, or iron, rake further breaks up dirt and levels it. After planting, the narrow, serrated blade of a scuffle hoe breaks up packed soil and loosens weeds. An edging hoe's straight blade cuts through sod around walks and flower beds.

□ WEEDING. The weed wand is a syringe-like device that injects herbicide into a weed's roots. Large-scale weed clearing requires a weed trimmer, a gasoline- or electric-powered machine with a whipping nylon line that mows weeds or grass tufts. A spring-steel lawn rake sweeps up light debris, such as dead weeds and grass trimmings.

□ SPRAYING. A garden-hose sprayer dilutes a concentrated solution as it squirts out of a nozzle. A slide-pump sprayer, with its 30-foot range, can be used beyond the reach of a hose. Caution: Keep separate, labeled sprayers for fertilizer and for insecticide or herbicide.

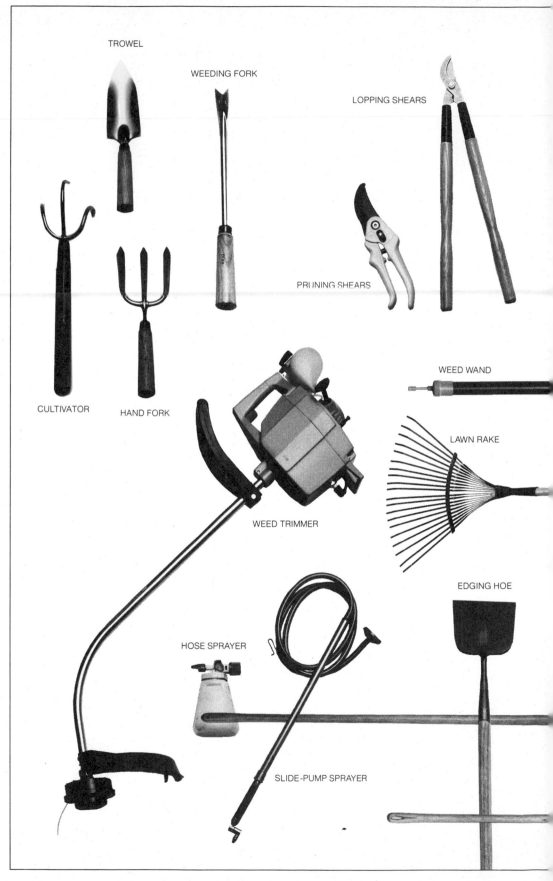

TROWEL

WEEDING FORK

LOPPING SHEARS

PRUNING SHEARS

CULTIVATOR

HAND FORK

WEED TRIMMER

WEED WAND

LAWN RAKE

EDGING HOE

HOSE SPRAYER

SLIDE-PUMP SPRAYER

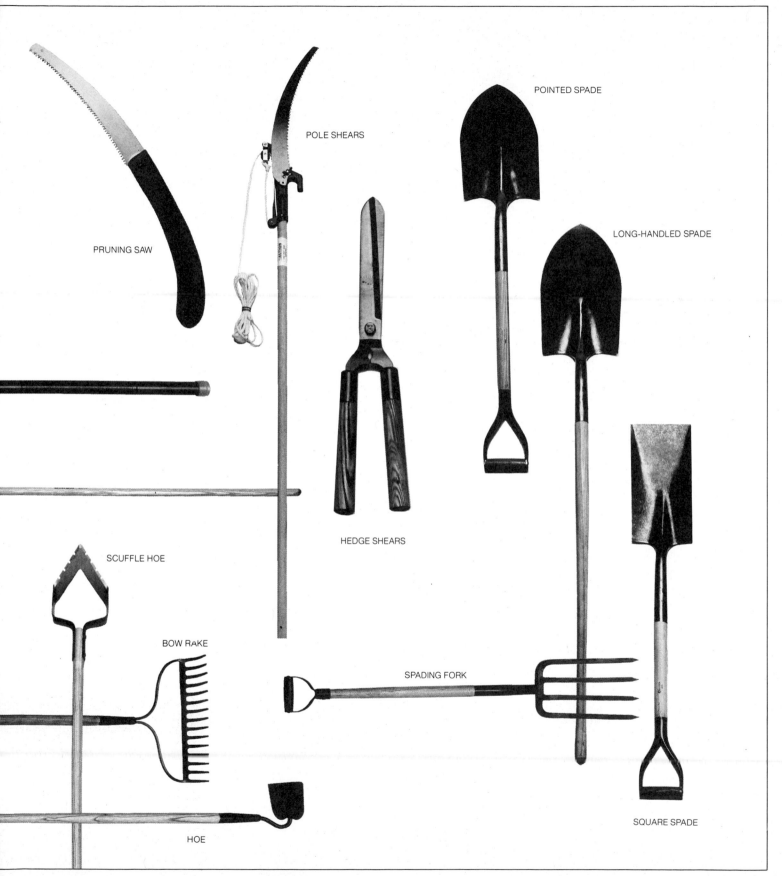

PRUNING SAW

POLE SHEARS

POINTED SPADE

LONG-HANDLED SPADE

HEDGE SHEARS

SCUFFLE HOE

BOW RAKE

SPADING FORK

SQUARE SPADE

HOE

Special Tools for Rare Jobs

Landscaping tasks that come up infrequently may call for tools designed expressly for the job. Such single-purpose tools need not form part of your basic tool kit: Hand tools can be purchased cooperatively by several gardeners in a neighborhood; large tools and gasoline-powered machines are available by the hour from tool-rental agencies.

□ PRESSURIZED SPRAYER. Powered by a hand pump that compresses air over a liquid, this sprayer provides pin-point application of small amounts of solution.

□ DETHATCHING RAKE. Suitable for small yards, this double-sided rake has blunt teeth that comb the choking build-up of dead grass out of a lawn.

□ POWER DETHATCHER. Steel blades on a rotating shaft tear out thatch to a depth set by the operator.

□ ROOT-ZONE INJECTOR. After the injector is pushed into the ground, water from a hose dissolves solid fertilizer cartridges and trickles out of the spike's tip, bathing a tree's root system with nutrients.

□ BULB PLANTER. Simply a cylindrical spade, this tool extracts a core of soil, leaving a hole for bulbs or small plants.

□ MATTOCK. Combining the features of two lighter implements, this sturdy tool severs roots with an ax-shaped blade or loosens hard ground with a heavy hoe.

□ EARTH AUGER. This electric-drill bit bores deep holes in the ground for the application of dry fertilizer or other solid chemicals to a tree's roots.

□ LAWN ROLLER. Filled with hundreds of pounds of water, the hollow drum compacts soil to prepare it for grass.

□ POWER TILLER. This formidable machine breaks up packed soil or mixes compost and conditioners into the soil.

□ BROADCAST SPREADER. The broadcast spreader's hopper (boxlike here, cylindrical in the one shown on page 44) contains grass seed or fertilizer; the machine throws a wide arc of material forward as it is pushed over the ground. An alternative machine, the trough spreader, drops material directly upon the ground.

□ POWER AERATOR. Hollow spikes on a rolling drum extract small cores of sod from a lawn, leaving holes through which nutrients can penetrate hard-packed soil.

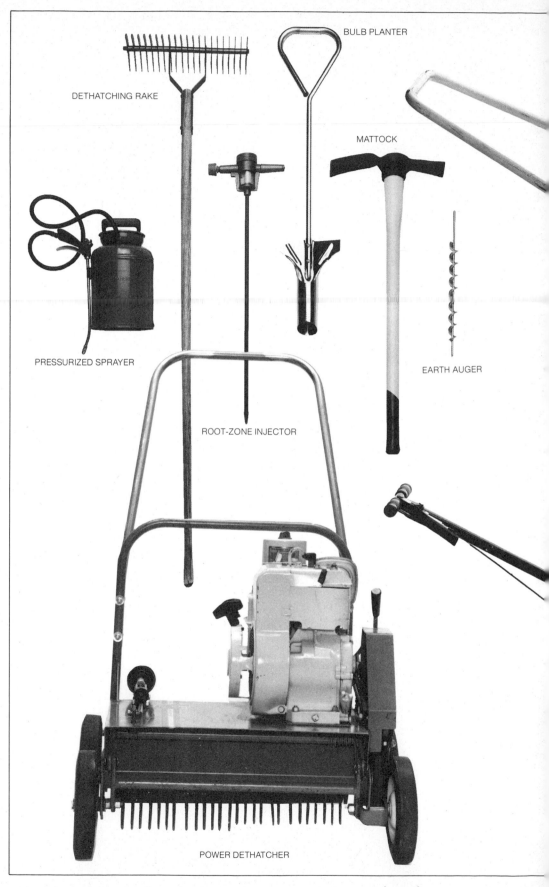

DETHATCHING RAKE

BULB PLANTER

MATTOCK

PRESSURIZED SPRAYER

EARTH AUGER

ROOT-ZONE INJECTOR

POWER DETHATCHER

LAWN ROLLER

POWER TILLER

BROADCAST SPREADER

POWER AERATOR

The Care and Repair of Landscaping Tools

A collection of gardening equipment represents a substantial investment, which needs and deserves protection. Commonsense maintenance begins with periodic inspections to catch minor nicks and loose joints before they grow into major problems. At times, repairs are in order when handles break or hoses split; except for such inexpensive tools as trowels and bamboo rakes, a repair almost always costs less than a replacement.

How you store your tools in the shed, garage or basement is an important part of their maintenance. Keep all your tools in an indoor area relatively free of dust and of rust-producing moisture. A wall covering of pegboard fitted with strong hooks to hold tools by their handles is an ideal arrangement; it keeps sharp blades away from hard, damp floors and secures them within easy sight and reach. Roll garden hoses carefully and hang them on brackets. Label fertilizers, insecticides and herbicides and store them on high shelves, out of the reach of children. Rinse and dry a sprayer after each use to prevent contamination and corrosion.

Cleanliness is as important as order in maintenance and storage. Use a coarse brush and running water to get rid of mud; use steel-wool pads to remove rust from tools that were neglected over the winter. After cleaning dirt from a cutting tool, wipe the blade or blades with a soft, disposable cloth dampened with a few drops of light household oil. Lubricate shears and loppers with a drop of oil on hinges and a few more on springs, then work the oil in by opening and closing the blades several times.

Sharpening the cutting edges of tools is a major part of routine tool care. Even a spade is inefficient if it is blunt, making a backbreaking chore of chopping tough roots. Fortunately, such tools as shears, spades, hoes and mattocks do not require professional sharpening; you can give them a good cutting edge at home with a flat file, a whetstone or—for long, curved blades—a rounded scythe stone.

Garden hoses spring leaks even when used with care. Avoid the temptation to wrap electrical tape around a punctured section; the makeshift patch will hold temporarily, but water pressure will eventually stretch the tape and seepage will begin again. Bicycle-tire repair kits are sometimes effective for a rubber hose, but they contain a solvent that can actually dissolve one made of vinyl. The best solution is to slice out the leaking section, then splice the hose with a mending kit *(page 13)* available at hardware stores and garden shops. Make clean cuts with a sharp knife, then soak both of the cut ends in hot water for a few minutes; the heat softens the vinyl, making it easier to fit a hose end over the connector that comes with the kit.

For a loose or corroded hose-end fitting, use a replacement coupling. Installing the new coupling is simple, but be sure you have the right size and model. Hoses are sized by inside diameters; measure after cutting away the old coupling. Remember that a female coupling is connected to the water source, a male one to a nozzle or sprayer.

Sharpening Spades and Shears

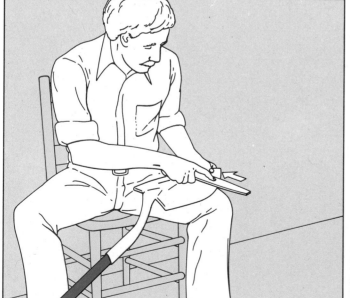

Putting a keen edge on a spade. Steady the spade on your knee, back side up, and stroke the edge of the spade with a flat file. Pull the file in long, steady strokes directed toward the center of the blade and following the angle of the bevel. If the inside edge of the blade is also beveled, turn the spade over and sharpen that edge.

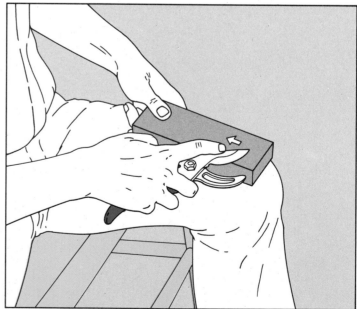

Honing a pair of shears. Set a whetstone on your knee, coarse side up, and pull the shears toward your body. Use only short, gentle strokes, and be sure to follow the bevel or bevels of each cutting blade. Then smooth out the sharpened blades by honing them on the fine-grained side of the whetstone.

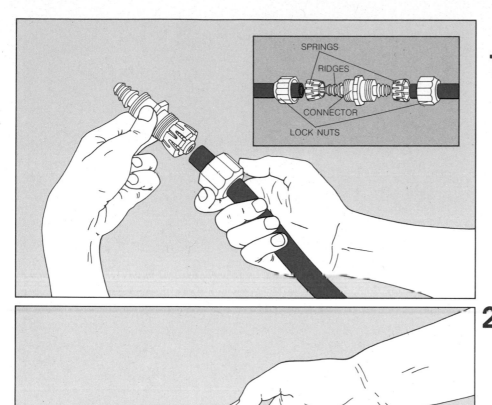

Mending a Leaky Hose

1 **Making the connection.** After cutting away the damaged section of the hose, slip one of the lock nuts from the mending kit *(inset)* over a cut end of the hose, unthreaded end first. Push the larger end of an expanding spring over the three ridges at one end of the connector; then, for a hose with a ½- or ⅝-inch inside diameter, insert the first ridge of the connector into the hose *(left)*. For hoses more than ⅝ inch in diameter, the connector must be pushed deeper into the hose; consult the manufacturer's instructions for more exact directions.

2 **Assembling the parts.** Slide the lock nut over the spring, and tighten the nut securely by hand (metal tools can damage the plastic connector). Finally, fasten the other end of the connector to the hose and tighten it.

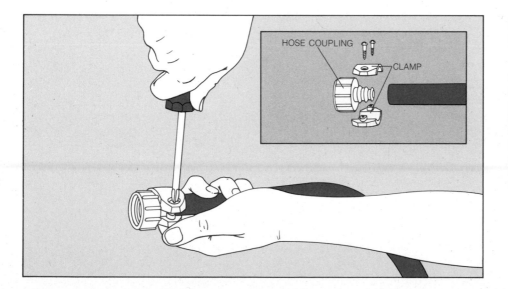

Replacing a Hose Coupling

Clamping a coupling in place. After cutting off the defective coupling, push the new coupling as far into the cut end of the hose as it will go. Then assemble the halves of the clamp around the hose and the base of the coupling *(inset)*. Match the holes in one half of the clamp with the screw receptacles in the other, then screw the halves together to tighten the clamp around the hose *(left)*.

Keeping a Canister Sprayer Clean

1 **Clearing the outlet holes.** Wearing rubber gloves to prevent contact with any chemical residue, unscrew the spray-directing tube and nozzle from the pistol grip (*inset*). Clear clogs and debris from the outlet holes at the end of the tube with a stiff wire, then wrap the wire in paper and dispose of it immediately to make certain that it will not be used again.

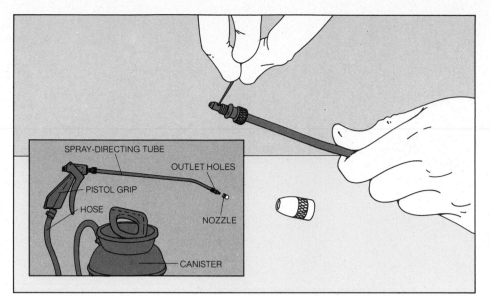

SPRAY-DIRECTING TUBE
OUTLET HOLES
PISTOL GRIP
HOSE
NOZZLE
CANISTER

2 **Cleaning the nozzle and tube.** Wipe the inside of the nozzle and the threads of the spray-directing tube with moistened cotton-tipped swabs until the cotton comes away clean, then lubricate the inside of the nozzle and the ends of the tube with a swab dipped in light household oil. Finally, lubricate the plastic O-rings at the ends of the tube to keep them from sticking and to prolong their sealing power.

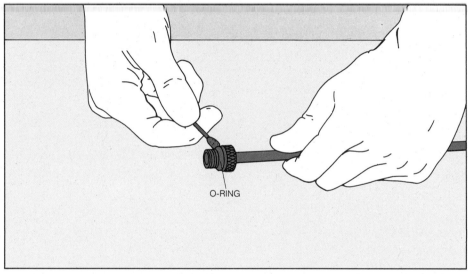

O-RING

Cleaning a Garden-hose Sprayer

Back-flushing the sprayer head. Wearing rubber gloves, rinse the reservoir of the sprayer with clear water, and connect the sprayer head to a garden hose. Turn the control valve of the head to ON, cover the outlet hole with a finger and run water through the hose; the clean water will flush back through and out of the suction tube, washing away chemical residues. Remove your finger from the outlet hole and run water through the sprayer in the normal direction; if the hole is clogged, clear it with stiff wire.

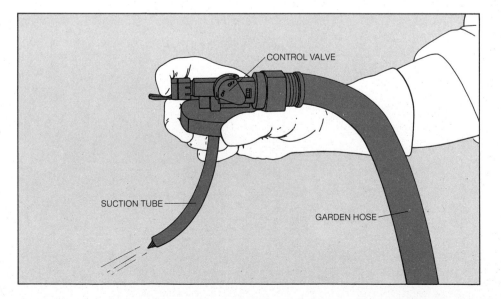

CONTROL VALVE
SUCTION TUBE
GARDEN HOSE

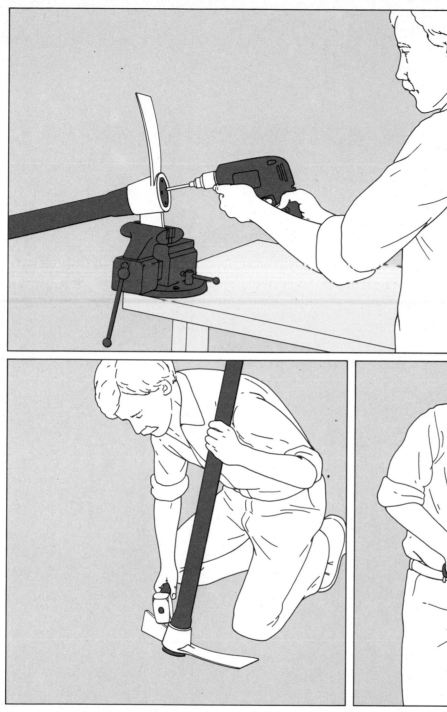

A New Handle for a Large Tool

1 **Removing a damaged handle.** Secure the head of a large tool, such as the mattock shown at left, in a metalworker's vise. Drill four deep holes into the wood at the top of the handle, using an electric drill with a ¼-inch bit; locate the holes as close as possible to the collar. Remove the tool from the vise, and tap the head with a small sledge hammer, driving it down toward the narrow part of the handle. If the head remains stuck, drill additional holes and tap more vigorously.

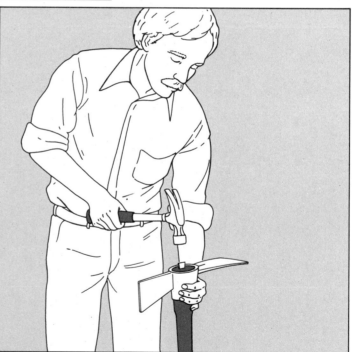

2 **Setting the new handle in place.** Hold the new handle upright on the floor, top down, then slip the mattock head down the handle. Drive the head into position with a small sledge hammer, forcing it over the wide section at the top of the handle; as you work, alternate the hammer blows from one side of the collar to the other to keep the head level.

When the head and handle are solidly joined, set the tool, head down, in warm water overnight to swell the wooden handle for a tighter fit.

3 **Making a tight fit.** Let the wood dry, then drive a ½-inch metal wedge, available at hardware stores, into the top of the handle. If the head of the tool is even slightly loose on the handle, drive additional wedges—perpendicular to the first—until the head is absolutely secure.

How to Be Your Own Landscape Designer

Like any other home improvement, landscaping calls for advance planning. Even a small yard is amazingly flexible, and the design imposed upon a yard is dictated largely by personal tastes and individual needs. Be prepared, then, to experiment on paper, weighing alternative solutions to your problems and sketching numerous possible designs. A thorough job in the planning stage not only assures you of a yard in which you can take pride and pleasure, but also saves the time and money it takes to compensate for decisions too hastily made.

Begin by evaluating the existing yard. A map of the property, such as the example at top opposite, is all but indispensable at this stage. In your map, include all the elements suggested in the example. If necessary, make a few phone calls for essential items of information. If you do not already have a plot plan that defines the shape and size of your property, you may be able to find one at the city or county recorder's office. Local utility companies will indicate the locations of underground lines and cables that might interfere with construction projects; in some communities this information is available from a service listed as "Miss Utility" in the white pages of the telephone book. If you are not sure of the directions of prevailing summer and winter winds, call the local weather service.

With a clear picture of the yard, you can determine the changes or additions that must be made to meet your needs. Draw up a list of these needs, based upon the activities you plan for the yard. Most yards are used for a variety of purposes—work, play, relaxation—and the best yards contain distinct areas for activities that might conflict. The map at bottom, opposite, shows outlines for several use areas, located according to

a universally accepted rule of residential landscape design: The most logical spot for an outdoor use area is next to the part of the house from which the area will be entered.

To some extent, the orientation of a house on its lot defines these areas. Traditionally, the house divides the lot into an approach area in the front yard; a private living area in the back; and an out-of-the-way service area, perhaps at the side of the house, for such storage facilities as a toolshed or a set of trash cans. A logical place for decoration would be the approach area at the front door, where passersby and arriving guests can appreciate it. A storage and utility area would be situated near a garage; a patio or deck for outdoor relaxation might be located directly outside French doors leading from the living room to the backyard. An area for games, on the other hand, should obviously be situated as far as possible from a pair of French doors.

Once you have chosen and outlined use areas on your map, experiment with preliminary designs for each one. Keep your plans fairly general at this stage; for example, if you decide to plant shrubs or a hedge in or around an area, think of them simply as tall or short, and as green or colorful, rather than stopping to choose a particular variety. Selecting the specific plants is the last step in the design process, and this step is best undertaken with the aid of the charts on pages 54, 61, 63, 82-83, 94-95 and 115, at a point when you know exactly what you want to accomplish with your new plantings.

As you consider these preliminary plans, look for strategic deployments and placements of plantings and construction projects to solve specific problems. If, like most people, you value pri-

vacy, place hedges, trees or fences as screens against the street and neighboring houses. Consider physical comfort in planning every area: The blazing afternoon sun, for example, will make a patio too bright and hot to sit on for part of the day, but a strategically placed tree will filter light and lower the temperature beneath its branches by 15 to 20° F. A high hedge or a few evergreens will shelter a walkway from fierce winter winds.

Think about convenience and safety. A frequently traveled path should be at least 4½ feet wide, to accommodate two people walking side by side. Set shrubs slightly back from walkway edges so that they will not snag clothing or shower passersby with dew. Paths should be well lighted for safety, and paving should be fairly level.

Consider maintenance, too. Hedges on both sides of a path may hinder snow removal in the winter; shrubs that grow too tall or too fast may need deep and frequent pruning to prevent them from blocking a view you want to preserve.

Finally, consider the yard as an esthetic object. To decide which views to enhance and which to block, tour the house interior, looking through every window, and check the views from a variety of vantage points in the yard itself. Then experiment with several arrangements of plantings and constructions, using sketches like the one at the top of page 18. Your own taste, of course, is the best guide to follow, but you should be aware of certain principles of design that professional landscape architects generally follow (pages 18-21). Used separately and in combination, in traditional or unconventional styles, these design concepts will help you to create a yard that is not only comfortable and functional, but a pleasure to the eye.

Planning the Design

1 Mapping the site. On a sheet of graph paper, with each square representing 1 square foot, draw a map of the lot and a floor plan of the ground floor of the house and any other existing structures. In the example at right, double lines represent walls, single vertical or horizontal lines represent windows, and single angled lines represent doors.

In mapping the area outside the house, mark downspout locations; avoid positioning flower beds or paved walkways at these points. Indicate good and bad views as seen from the windows and from several places in the yard; among these views, include the positions of neighbors' yards and houses. Draw in existing trees, shrubs, flower beds and underground utilities; note such characteristics of the terrain as steep banks, level areas and spots with good drainage. Finally, indicate the position of the sun at morning, midday and late afternoon, and the direction of prevailing summer and winter winds.

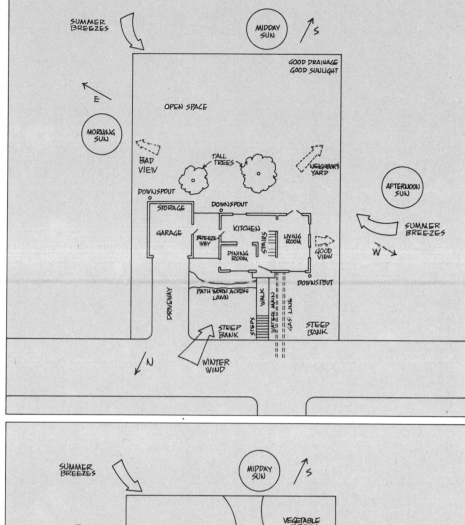

2 Outlining use areas. On tracing paper taped over the basic map of the house and lot, outline use areas for the major sections of the yard. (For simplicity in the example at right, only the lettering on the tracing paper is shown; in actuality, the lettering on the map would be visible through the overlay.) In the plan shown here, space accessible from both the living room and the kitchen becomes an outdoor living and dining area. The expanse of lawn behind the garage is set aside as a play area; game equipment can be stored in the garage. A back corner of the lot with good drainage and sunlight is reserved as a vegetable garden, with storage space for garden tools in an adjacent utility area.

Smaller areas at the front of the house are also assigned functions, fully depicted in the final plan at the top of page 18. The portion of the lawn bordered by the street and the driveway becomes the main approach area, and the steep bank that leads to the street is devoted to decorative plantings to block the view of the street from the living-room and dining-room windows.

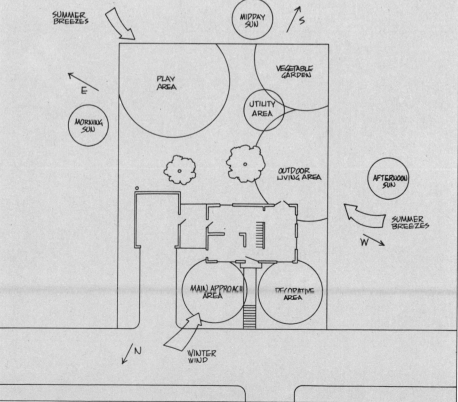

3 Experimenting with designs. Tape a fresh sheet of tracing paper over your map, and experiment with designs for each of the use areas. In the example shown here, the outdoor living and dining area becomes a paved patio; new shade trees and a high hedge on the rim of the patio block the afternoon sun and the view of the neighbor's yard. The play area is left open, except for a border hedge between the yard and another undesirable view. The vegetable garden in the rear corner of the lot is bordered by fences and a flower bed; a toolshed and a row of shrubs separate the garden from the patio.

New, more efficient traffic patterns are established by a steppingstone path between the garage door and the play area and by a paved walkway leading from the end of the path to the patio. In the front yard, another paved walkway runs from the driveway to the front door, replacing the old footpath worn across the grass and eliminating the need for a walkway between the door and the street. Decorative, permanent ground cover replaces hard-to-mow grass on the steep bank facing the street; the trees that block the view of the street from the house help to beautify the new approach.

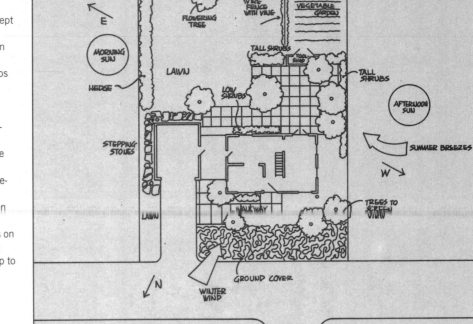

Principles of Landscape Design

Unity and balance. To meet one basic design objective, related elements in a yard are arranged to create a unified picture, in which the viewer's eye travels easily over all the plantings. In such a design (*top right*), no single element stops the eye; instead, colors, textures and shapes are coordinated to blend and contrast as part of a larger picture, and the ensemble has a continuous, graceful silhouette.

The best way to assess the balance of a landscape is to picture it as a framed view divided vertically in half. A well-balanced design attracts your eye equally to each half; neither side will overpower the other. The halves of a symmetrically balanced design (*middle*) are almost mirror images; in an asymmetrically balanced view (*bottom*), the halves are different, but the sizes and shapes of the elements in each half are enough alike to draw the eye equally to both sides.

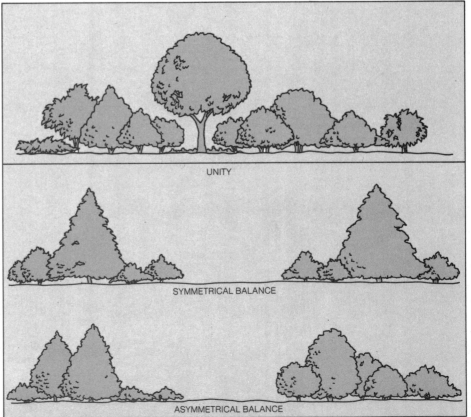

UNITY

SYMMETRICAL BALANCE

ASYMMETRICAL BALANCE

Focal point and proportion. Within a landscape design, a single element called the focal point may be used to attract the eye; no view should have more than one focal point. For a front-yard design *(below),* the front door of the house is commonly used as a focal point, and is traditionally framed by arrangements of ornamental trees, shrubs or flowers that draw the eye toward the point of interest.

The term "proportion" refers to the relationships among the sizes of the plants and buildings in a landscape design. No set rule controls these sizes, but a height-to-width ratio of 5 to 3 between neighboring elements is generally pleasing. Thus, in the example at bottom, the tree is in proportion with the house to its left, but is too tall for the house at the right.

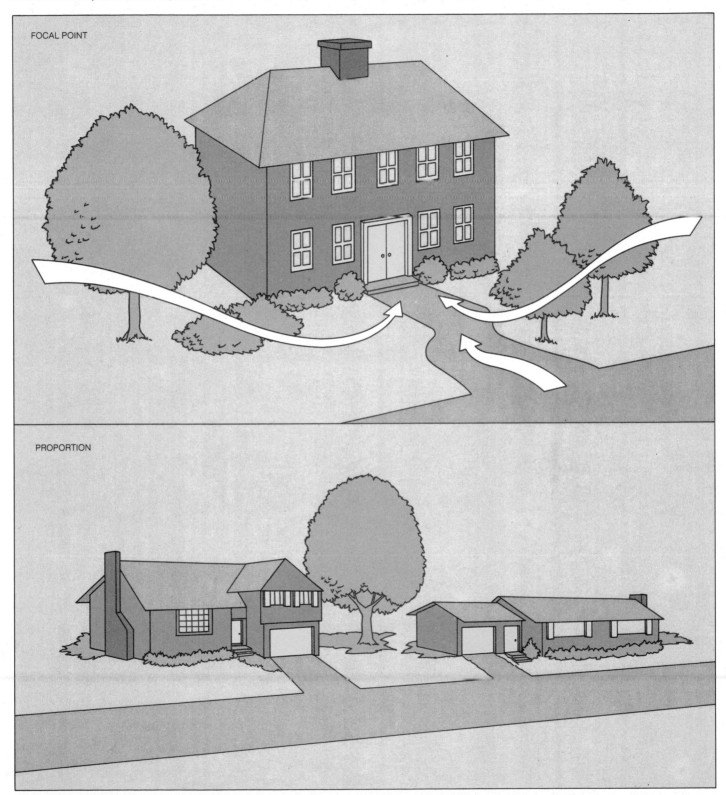

FOCAL POINT

PROPORTION

Rhythm and allure. The repeated use of similar patterns or shapes creates a visual rhythm in a landscape design; the repetition stimulates a sense of movement by drawing the eye from one point or area to the next. In the example at top right, the openness and clarity of rectangular paving blocks and planting beds create a simple, easily grasped rhythm.

The term ''allure'' refers to the element of surprise in a design and to devices that entice the viewer to explore a landscape. The example at bottom contains two such strategies. When viewed from the yard, the hidden corner of the house stimulates a viewer's curiosity about that area; when viewed from the house, the fence partially covered by ivy hides a surprise—a small stone terrace and a fountain.

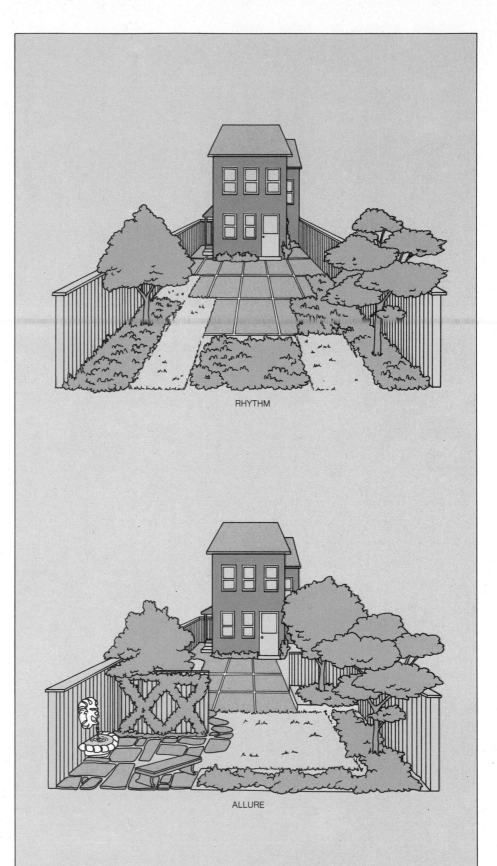

RHYTHM

ALLURE

Designing with geometrical shapes. Plantings and paving arranged in common, recognizable shapes give a landscape orderliness and predictability—two features that are pleasing to the eye. Rectangles and squares (*below, top*) reflect and extend the architectural lines of a house. Circles and curves (*middle*) add a different kind of interest to a pattern by counterbalancing and contrasting the straight lines of the house. Triangles draw the eye to a focal point—in the example at bottom, to the expanse of lawn at the center of the yard.

RECTANGLES AND SQUARES

CIRCLES AND CURVES

TRIANGLES

Moving Earth to Reshape the Lay of the Land

The unpatterned rise and roll of a naturally sloping terrain is attractive—from a distance. Except for the most rustic setting, however, irregular troughs and ridges are generally undesirable in a yard. They hamper drainage, so that lawn and garden care becomes a frustrating chore rather than a pleasant pastime; moreover, bumps and slopes make unsuitable foundations for patios or play areas. Reshaping the lay of uneven land is often an essential preliminary to a landscaping or construction project.

Shown on the following pages are techniques that transform a broken, uninviting yard into a nearly level space suitable for lawns, shrubs and trees. To begin with, sharp inclines are leveled or terraced to prevent plantings at the base of a slope from being drowned by the runoff of a heavy rain. Then the newly leveled areas must be gently graded: Water will pool on perfectly level land, drowning fragile plants and flowers and making yard work impractical for several days after a downpour.

For most sites, the gentlest slope that will provide adequate drainage is 1 inch of rise for each 4 feet of horizontal run. If different parts of your yard slope naturally in different directions, wait for a steady, heavy rain and observe the natural drainage patterns for an hour or so. After the weather clears, use the string-and-grid method (page 25) to establish the right grade for each part of the yard.

Although some earth-moving jobs are extensive enough to warrant hiring an excavating company, a surprising amount of earth can be moved by hand, in short sessions of digging and hauling. If you do choose to undertake an excavating project, you will need a pair of sturdy shoes with heavy, treaded soles to ensure good footing and to pad the soles of your feet

against the top of a spade blade. You will also need a pointed spade for skimming sod (page 24) and digging the soil and a heavy metal rake with a flat top for graining and smoothing the earth. Several stakes, a ball of string and a line level are necessary to set the slope of your plot and mark any grade changes.

To economize effort, work when the soil is slightly moist: Wet soil is much heavier—and therefore more difficult to move—than barely moist dirt, while arid soil can be rock-hard and unyielding, even to the sharpened blade of a steel tool. A project that requires you to move only a small amount of earth from one place to another will simplify and ease the grading job; for example, you might prefer to rough-grade a slope and prevent erosion by digging a few trenches for wooden baffles (page 26), rather than undertake the large-scale and laborious job of building a retaining wall (pages 28-31).

To avoid a strained back—the most common injury in this type of work—use your arms and legs as well as your back to lift a shovel (opposite). Use a wheelbarrow or other lifting aid whenever practical to transfer earth from one spot to another or to lift heavy loads.

If a job seems more than you can handle yourself, do all you can in advance to lighten the work load and lessen the cost of the hired excavators. Put up fences around areas you do not want disturbed; inexpensive snow fencing, which comes in large rolls and can be easily erected, is a good choice. Keep all heavy equipment out of actual or potential garden beds; the weight of the machines can compact the soil to a depth of 4 feet, rendering it impervious to water and useless for planting. When fencing in trees, include enough ground to protect their root sys-

tems. Finally, keep children and pets out of the way of workers, and clear your yard and driveway of any obstacles that block access to the work area.

Regardless of who does the actual digging, it is your responsibility to locate any electric, telephone or sewer lines beneath your land. If necessary, request local utility agencies to mark these lines before the earthmovers arrive.

To balance cuts and fills, professional excavators often make a survey or map of differences in elevation and soil volume, then systematically bring cavities up to grade with earth taken from ridges and hillocks. Few of the backyard digging projects that you can tackle yourself are extensive enough to warrant the expense of such a survey, but you may discover midway through the work that you have too much or too little soil and must pay someone to cart soil away or deliver more.

If professional excavators are reshaping your yard, agree upon the disposal of excess soil before digging begins. Some contractors take it as part of their job to remove the excess, while others tack on an additional fee; moreover, you may want to keep any extra soil for use elsewhere on your property.

If you must purchase earth to top off a grade, be sure to gauge your order according to your needs: A cubic yard of soil will cover 300 square feet of ground to a depth of 1 inch. Buy topsoil—a mix of earth and fertilizers from which stones, wood chips and weeds have been removed—rather than fill, which often contains rocks and dense chunks of rock-riddled clay. Ask a local nursery for the names of reputable soil dealers in your area; topsoil of poor quality may be contaminated by invisible weed seeds, disease germs and fungus spores.

The Right Way to Wield a Spade

A four-stage action. Standing upright, set your foot atop the blade of the spade *(first picture)* and force the blade deep into the earth. Step back, set your hands in the positions shown in the second picture, and force the top of the handle down, using the tool as a lever to dislodge the soil. Bend forward from the waist, flexing your knees, and slide your lower hand down the handle for better leverage; then, using arms, back and legs together, lift and pitch the soil *(third and fourth pictures)*. To save strength, work slowly and avoid overloading the spade.

Managing Heavy Loads with Minimal Strain

A two-hand lift. Holding your torso erect, squat as close as possible to the load to be lifted *(far left)*. Holding the load close to your body, stand up slowly *(center)*; in this stage of the lift, keep your pelvis tucked forward and use your legs—not your back—for lifting force. To lessen strain on your back, continue to hold the load close to your waist *(right)*, and move your entire body, not just your torso, when you turn.

A one-hand lift. Bending your knees slightly and keeping your back straight, lean forward from the waist to reach the load *(far left)*. Using your legs for lifting power and keeping your shoulders level, raise your body upright to lift the load; when carrying the load, extend your free arm for balance *(right)*.

Clearing logs from a site. To move a long, evenly cylindrical log, push it onto and across three or four rollers made of wood or of iron pipe. Tie a rope around the forward end of the log and pull it slowly over the rollers; as each roller comes free in back of the log, move it to the front.

Moving rocks and stumps. Using a sturdy, rigid rod, lever large stones, stumps or other unwieldy weights onto a sheet of heavy canvas or burlap. Grasp the cloth firmly at both corners of one end and drag the object from the site.

Leveling and Grading a Plot of Land

1 Skimming sod from the surface. Hold a pointed spade almost parallel to the ground and work it in short, jabbing strokes to separate the sod from underlying soil. After clearing off the sod, use the spade to scrape the soil off to a depth of 1 inch to remove roots that might later send up new, unwanted shoots.

2 Leveling ridges and depressions. After clearing away the sod, transfer the dirt from obvious high spots in the plot to low spots. After you drop each load, use the end of the blade to break the soil into chunks 1 inch wide or less.

3 **Setting a slope with stakes and strings.** Drive stakes at the four corners of the plot; the stakes at the lowest points (generally farthest from the house) should be tall enough to set their tops roughly level with those at the highest points. Tie a string to one of the higher stakes and stretch it along the side of the plot to a lower stake. As a helper checks a line level hung from the string, raise or lower the string as necessary to level it. Mark the lower stake at the level of the string, then move the string down this stake to set the desired slope (*page 22*) and tie it to the stake.

Repeat the procedure on the other side of the plot, then complete the boundary by tying leveled strings between the stakes at the top and the bottom of the plot.

4 **Laying out a grid.** Drive stakes at 6-foot intervals just outside the strings that mark the boundaries of the plot, then make a grid over the area by tying a string between each opposite pair of stakes at the level of the boundary strings. Make sure the strings are taut; if necessary, smooth the soil beneath them for clearance between the strings and the ground.

5 **Grading the surface.** Working in one 6-foot square at a time, use a heavy rake to break up the soil to the consistency of coarse sand and spread it parallel to the plane of the string grid. Finally, smooth the plot with the flat top side of the rake; remove the stakes and strings.

Correcting Faulty Drainage

To professional landscapers, the term "drainage" has two meanings: the seepage of water into the soil and the flow of water over a particular stretch of land. Faulty drainage of either sort can frustrate even the most hardworking homeowner. Soil that is too porous does not hold water long enough for plants to absorb it; soil that is too dense keeps water on the surface of the ground, depriving plant roots of the periodic soaking they require. In another problem of surface drainage, water that flows rapidly down a steep slope erodes the soil, exposing plant roots on the face of the slope and drowning or washing away plants at the foot of the slope.

To gauge soil porosity, dig a hole 2 feet deep and fill it with water. If the water disappears in 24 hours or less, the soil is too porous; if any water is still visible after 48 hours, the soil is too dense. Both problems are solved in the same way—by adding an organic amendment such as peat moss, manure or compost to alter the consistency of the soil (page 32).

Water flow on an incline can be controlled by grading the surface (page 22), but reshaping an entire slope is often impractical for large areas, and it is destructive in places where valued plantings are thriving. Other effective remedies available to the homeowner include the baffles, berms and swales, and terraces shown on these pages.

Baffles, consisting of steplike obstructions set into a hillside, slow runoff by repeatedly interrupting the flow of water down a slope. The obstructions can be assembled with treated timbers or railroad ties, like those used to build the retaining wall shown on page 29, or built up with large stones. They should be arranged in a series of neat rows, one above another, and set at a slight downward incline to prevent rain water from pooling along them after a downpour.

Artificial ridges and depressions called berms and swales, another means of slowing the downward flow of water, offer the added advantage of channeling the water away from an object or area at the foot of a slope. The berms, essentially low earthen dams mounded below shallow trenches, or swales, catch the water and divert it across the hillside. To moderate the broken, washboard-like appearance of berms and swales, you can plant vines or other kinds of ground cover directly upon them.

Sculpting a slope into one or more low terraces is a somewhat more drastic way of slowing erosive runoff. To build terraces you must excavate the slope, much as you would in building a retaining wall (page 28), but each excavation need be no more than 18 inches high. The plateau below a drop-off stops the descending water, then releases it for a slow roll to the next drop-off.

Slowing runoff with baffles. Dig a series of trenches 4 inches deep in a zigzag pattern across the face of a hillside; locate the trenches about 3 feet apart, and extend the high end of each trench about 6 inches beyond the low end of the trench above it. Using stakes, a string and a line level as shown on page 25, Step 3, establish a slope of 1 inch for every 4 feet of a trench run. Cut timbers to fit the trenches (page 30, Step 2), drill ⅜-inch holes through the ends and the middle of each timber, and spike the timbers into the ground with 1-foot lengths of ⅜-inch steel reinforcing rod.

Channeling runoff with berms and swales. Dig a trench, or swale, as wide as a spade and 3 inches deep, locating it above and alongside the area you wish to protect. As you dig, pile the soil about 6 inches below the swale to form a ridge, or berm. Tamp the loose soil of the berm to form a gently undulating surface between the swale and the berm.

Terracing a slope. Drive a pair of stakes into the hillside about 18 inches above the foot of the slope, then stretch and level a string between the stakes (*above, left*). At this line, cut a horizontal shelf into the slope, pitching the excavated earth just below the line to extend the shelf forward (*above, right*). About 18 inches above the drop-off, build a second shelf in the same way; work your way up the hill, sculpting the earth with excavations and shelves, until you reach the top. Finally, grade each shelf slightly downward so that water will not puddle or pool.

A Barrier of Weatherproof Wood

Retaining walls of rough-hewn or finished timbers have long been used by farmers to transform steep, useless hillsides into tillable cropland. Nowadays they are also valued by homeowners as an element in landscape planning, lending charm to yards and gardens.

The farmer's and homeowner's walls differ in size and construction as well as function: A retaining wall designed to reclaim land is usually a massive, complex structure. By contrast, the simplified design shown on these pages is easy to build, yet sturdy; it presents a trim face, unmarked by nails or fasteners, and in most localities it requires no building permit. Though adequate for most landscaping projects, this design should not be used for walls rising more than 3 feet above the ground; higher walls require greater reinforcement, a more elaborate drainage system and, in most cases, both a building permit and the services of a structural engineer.

Wooden retaining walls can be made of any timbers that have been treated to resist rot and termites. Railroad ties were the material of choice in times past, when they were inexpensive and easy to come by. Nowadays, however, most landscapers and homeowners use other lumber, since railroad ties are scarcer and more costly than before—and also because they are treated with the preservative creosote, which is poisonous to many plants. Pressure-treated timbers of poplar or pine, rough- or smooth-sawed and 6 inches square or 6 by 8 inches in cross section, are excellent alternatives. They come in convenient 8- and 12-foot lengths and are treated with preservatives that are harmless to plants. Redwood, a popular choice for all outdoor construction, is as durable as pressure-treated timbers but more expensive.

To anchor a retaining wall solidly, you must dig a trench deep enough to bury the first course of timbers. Plan this trench carefully; if possible, locate it about midway up the slope, so that soil from the trench and the area below the wall can be used to level or gently grade the ground behind the wall. If you build the wall near the bottom of the slope, you will probably need to purchase fill; if you place the wall near the top of the slope, you may need to have some excess soil carried away.

Before you begin to excavate soil, ask your local utility agencies whether there are underground electric, telephone or sewer lines at your digging site. If any of these lines run within 4 feet of the surface, have them marked by the appropriate agency and place your wall well away from the mark.

When you have excavated the trench for the bottom timbers, use a chain saw to cut them to fit the span. Follow commonsense rules of safety in using the saw: Be sure the cutting teeth are sharp and the chain is at the proper tension and well lubricated. Steady the timbers on solid supports for sawing, and chalk cutting lines on the timbers as guides. Wear goggles to protect your eyes from flying wood chips. Brace the saw firmly on the ground before starting it, and hold the saw with both hands when cutting.

In addition to the chain saw, you will need a heavy, long-handled sledge hammer and a lighter hand sledge; an electric drill with ⅛-inch and ⅜-inch bits; two 42-inch-long bars of reinforcing steel (commonly known as rebar) for every 8 feet of the first course of timbers; about four 8-inch galvanized spikes for every 8 feet of each course above the first; and two 8-inch spikes for each reinforcing timber, or deadman.

Anatomy of a retaining wall. Set in a shallow trench, this wooden retaining wall rises 2 feet above the ground in five courses of 6-by-6-inch timbers. The bottom, buried course is anchored in the ground by lengths of reinforcing steel; each successive course is secured to the one below it with spikes, which are toe-nailed from behind to leave the face of the wall smooth and unmarked. In the second course, 1-inch gaps are left between adjacent timbers to permit water to drain from the ground behind the wall. From the third course, reinforcing timbers called deadmen, spaced at 6-foot intervals, project 4 feet back into the soil to help the wall resist the pressure of the retained earth.

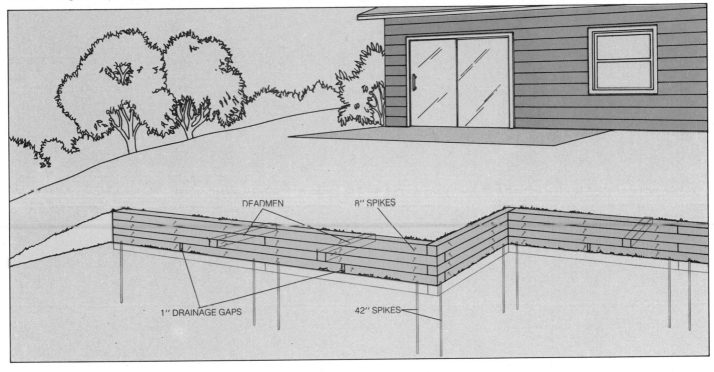

DEADMEN   8" SPIKES

1" DRAINAGE GAPS   42" SPIKES

Building the Wall

1 Excavating the site. Working upward from the base of the slope, cut away the earth along the path of the wall with a pick and shovel. Pitch the excavated soil behind the site of the wall to create a plateau, leaving a drop-off slightly lower than the planned height of the wall. Tamp the apron of earth in front of the drop-off.

2 **Setting a level base.** Drive stakes to mark the ends of each straight wall section, stretch strings between the stakes and level the strings with a line level. Below each string, dig a trench about 1 foot wide and 6 inches deep, measuring frequently down from the string to be sure that the bottom of the trench is level. Remove the stakes and strings.

With a chain saw, cut timbers at least 6 feet long to fit the trench. Drill ⅜-inch holes through the timbers, 6 inches from each end.

3 **Putting in the first course.** Lay a course of the cut timbers end to end in the trench; to make a corner, butt the end of one timber at a right angle to the side of another. With a sledge hammer, drive 42-inch bars of ⅜-inch reinforcing steel through the drilled holes in the timbers and into the ground. At each bar location, mark the backs of the timbers with chalk; avoid these locations when you secure the next course.

4 **Adding a second course.** Lay the second course of the wall, leaving 1-inch drainage gaps between the ends of adjacent timbers; cut and arrange the second-course timbers so that these gaps do not lie over the joints of the first course. Every 2 feet along the wall, bore ⅛-inch pilot holes, starting midway up the backs of the timbers and angling the holes downward at about 60°; then toenail the second course to the first by driving 8-inch galvanized spikes into the pilot holes with a hand sledge.

5 Excavating for the deadmen. At points about 6 feet apart along the wall, dig 4-foot-long troughs back into the hillside, making the bottom of each trough level with the top of the second course. Be sure to dig the outermost troughs at least 3 feet in from the ends of the wall, so that the deadmen at these locations will be concealed by retained soil.

6 Seating a deadman. Lay each deadman in its trough, with the outer end resting on the second course, flush to the front of the wall. Kneel or crouch a few feet in front of the wall and sight along each deadman timber as a rough test of levelness. If the back end is too high, scoop some earth out of the trough; add soil if the back end is too low. After leveling a deadman timber, toenail it to the second course with two 8-inch spikes driven through opposite sides.

7 Completing the wall. Cut timbers to fit between the deadmen, and spike them into place as a third course. Nail squares of galvanized screening over the backs of the drainage gaps. Then shovel excavated soil behind the wall up to the third course, compact the soil with a tamper and fill the deadman troughs. From this point, continue building the wall upward, one course at a time, to the top timbers. Finally, fill the space behind the wall with soil.

Last Step before Planting: Preparing the Soil

Few experiences are as disheartening as watching the best parts of a newly planted landscape wither and die. Yet such a disaster is eminently preventable. When large groups of plants fail to flourish, the reason is likely to be either a failure to prepare the soil correctly or a failure to match the plants to the soil that has to sustain them.

All soil is composed of mineral particles of various sizes, ranging from fine, dense clay to coarse, loose sand; in addition, soil contains humus, a mixture of decayed animal and vegetable matter that acts as a fertilizer and is an important determinant of the soil's texture. Good garden soil is spongy enough to retain moisture but porous enough for good drainage and air circulation. It contains the nutrients needed for plant growth, most notably nitrogen, phosphorus and potassium. And it is neither too acid nor too alkaline—conditions that impair the ability of roots to extract nutrients from the soil.

The best soils, called loams, contain sand, clay and humus in roughly equal proportions. Few yards are naturally favored with such soil—but equally rare is soil so poor that it will destroy any plant put into it. And you can improve almost any soil by tilling and by incorporating so-called amendments, or additions.

The first step in soil improvement is testing the physical structure and the chemistry of the existing soil. If you have had difficulty growing plants in your yard in the past, it may be worthwhile contacting your county extension service and arranging to send in a soil sample for analysis. But you can usually get all the information you need by performing a few simple tests yourself.

Begin by assessing the structure of your soil—that is, its proportions of clay, sand and humus. Soil with too much clay is dense and heavy, slippery when wet, hard and lumpy when dry. Because it retains water almost indefinitely, clay is a prime cause of drainage problems. Sandy soil, which is light and gritty, tends to dry too quickly, so that plants are parched and nutrients are leached out.

For a detailed picture of soil components, perform the water test shown at near right; from it, you can accurately gauge the need for structure-improving amendments. To break up clayey soil, use coarse builder's sand, available at building-supply stores and some garden centers. Both sandy and clayey soils should be treated with organic matter, which makes sandy soils more spongy, clayey soils more porous. Peat moss and dehydrated manure, sold at garden centers, are the commonest amendments of this kind. But the best soil amendment, because it adds nutrients as well as improving structure, is compost, a rich, dark mixture of decayed animal and vegetable matter that you can prepare yourself in backyard storage piles (page 35).

To perform chemical tests, use an inexpensive soil-test kit, available at garden centers. The kit contains an array of test tubes and chemicals and a set of charts for interpreting the results. Each of the chemicals responds to a specific soil characteristic—typically, the quantity of nitrogen, potassium or phosphorus and the acidity or alkalinity of the soil, indicated by a pH number.

Neutral soil has a pH of 7, the midpoint in a pH scale that runs from 0 to 14. Above 7, soil is increasingly alkaline; below 7, increasingly acid. Most plants grow best in slightly acid soil, between 6.5 and 6.8. Some popular plants, such as azaleas and rhododendrons, prefer more acidity; others, such as lilacs and delphiniums, thrive on mild alkalinity. A pH test, used together with the plant charts on pages 54, 61, 63, 82-83, 94-95 and 115, will help you select the best plants for your soil. But some soil amendments are usually needed as well, particularly in rainy, humid climates, which tend to produce excessively acid soil, and in dry climates, which tend to produce alkalinity.

To reduce acidity, add lime to the soil. The simplest and safest type to apply is granular limestone, available as calcic limestone or—somewhat better—as dolomitic limestone, which has the advantage of adding a small amount of magnesium, an essential nutrient. In light, sandy soil, use 5 pounds of limestone for every 100 square feet; in heavy, clayey soil, increase the amount by one third.

Alkaline soil can be corrected with sulfur, available as pure ground sulfur, iron sulfate or aluminum sulfate. Pure sulfur acts more slowly than the others, but it lasts longer; iron sulfate adds iron to the soil, encouraging lush, dark foliage; aluminum sulfate, though readily available, must be used with special caution because an excess of aluminum is harmful to plants. To reduce the alkalinity of 100 square feet of light soil by a pH interval of .5 to 1, use 3 pounds of iron sulfate or aluminum sulfate or ½ pound of ground sulfur; for heavy soil, increase these amounts by one third.

The best time to test a soil and to improve its structure and pH rating is four to six months before planting, to give the amendments plenty of time to become thoroughly incorporated. Add organic matter and sand as you till the soil, then broadcast lime or sulfur on the surface, either directly from the bag or with a shovel, and rake it into the top few inches. Chemical fertilizers are usually added at planting time, so that rain water does not leach them out of the soil before plants can use them.

To till a large area quickly and easily, use a power tiller, available from tool-rental agencies. Your choice of a tiller depends largely upon your experience and special needs: A model with the engine mounted at the front and the tines set behind it is more stable and generally preferable for a beginner; a model with front-mounted tines is more maneuverable in tight places.

For a small area, manual tilling with a spade or spading fork may be a better choice; in fact, many professionals consider hand tilling preferable in preparing a garden bed, as opposed to a field for crops. The manual technique called double digging (page 34) is the most arduous but also the most thorough method of preparing the soil. Because it ensures good soil to a depth of nearly 20 inches, it is ideal for a new bed, especially one intended for deep-rooted perennials.

Whatever method you choose, do not till soggy soil, which breaks up into large, heavy clods that can dry as hard as rocks. To test for moisture, squeeze some soil in your hand; a sticky, compact mass that will not crumble is too wet. Three days after a rain, when the soil is neither too wet nor annoyingly dusty and dry, is generally a good time to till.

Analyzing the Structure and Chemistry of Soil

1 **Gathering samples.** At several different spots within the area you intend to plant, dig holes about 6 inches wide and one spade (6 to 8 inches) deep. Slice a thin wedge of soil from the wall of each hole, deposit the soil in a plastic bucket and mix the samples in the bucket with the spade or a trowel. Do not touch the soil samples with your hands.

Certain landscape features, particularly stone walls and foundations, shrubs and trees, can alter the pH of nearby soil. Test soil from each of these areas individually.

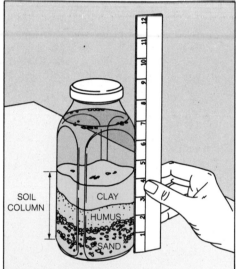

2 **Analyzing soil structure.** Fill a quart bottle half full of water, then add soil until the bottle is nearly full. Cap the bottle and shake it vigorously to mix the soil and water together.

Wait for the soil to settle; this will usually take about three hours. Then, using a ruler held alongside the bottle, measure the height of the settled soil. In the same way, measure the thickness of each layer: smooth, uniform clay at the top; darker topsoil and humus in the middle; sand and pebbles on the bottom. To determine the percentage of the soil represented by each component, divide each of these figures by the total height of the soil.

If your measurements show that the percentage of topsoil and organic matter is less than 25 per cent of the total, add peat moss, manure or compost. If the percentage of clay in the soil is greater than 25 per cent, plan to incorporate coarse sand as well as humus when you are tilling the ground (*page 34*). If the soil is more than 30 per cent sand, you will want to double the amount of added organic matter.

3 **Using a chemical test kit.** With a spoon, fill a test tube one-quarter full of soil, then add the amount of test chemical called for in the kit manual. Cap the test tube and shake it to mix the soil and the chemical thoroughly.

If your kit has a funnel and filter papers, filter out the soil; if not, let it settle completely.

Compare the color of the remaining solution to those on the appropriate test chart. In a chart for a test of chemical nutrients, each color indicates the percentage of a specific nutrient in the fertilizer you buy; for a pH test, each color represents a pH level. If the color of the solution falls between two colors on a chart, estimate a pH number between the two levels.

Improving Soil with Air and Amendments

Double digging. Outline the bed by driving a spade straight down into the earth with your foot, then cut parallel lines approximately 2 feet apart across the bed, marking off a series of rectangular digging sections. Dig out the soil from one of the end sections to the full depth of the spade (6 to 8 inches), depositing the soil outside the edge of the planting bed *(below, left)*. Next, spread a 3-inch-thick layer of soil

amendments in the bottom of the trench you have just made, then mix the amendments into the 8 inches of soil below them; use a mattock, if necessary, to break up the soil. Then fill this trench with soil from the adjacent digging section *(below, right)*, leaving a second trench that is roughly 2 feet wide and 8 inches deep. Dig another 3 inches of amendments into the soil that now fills the first section you dug up.

Spread amendments in the trench of the second section, dig them in, and transfer the top 8 inches of soil from the third section to fill up the second. When you have incorporated amendments into this soil, resume the process of incorporating amendments and transferring dirt until you reach the last section. Dig amendments into the last trench, then fill it with the soil from the first section and again dig in amendments.

Operating a power tiller. Set the controls of the tiller in neutral, position the machine at one corner of the planting bed, and set the tines to the correct depth for your soil—from 3 inches for heavy, clayey soil to 8 inches for sandy soil. Start the engine, then shift into forward and guide the machine along one side of the bed. When you reach the far end of the bed, make a broad turn and work back in the opposite direction, creating a U-shaped area of tilled soil; continue tilling back and forth in this way until you have moved across the entire bed *(inset)*. Then shift into neutral, move the tiller to the first untilled strip and repeat the tilling pattern until all the soil has been turned. For heavy soil, reset the tines at 6 inches and repeat the tilling pattern.

For the second stage of tilling, spread a 3-inch layer of such soil amendments as coarse sand and humus over the earth. Set the tiller tines at their maximum depth and work the amendments into the soil. Use the same tilling pattern as before, but work so that the second tilling lines are perpendicular to the first.

If the tiller bucks and jumps excessively, move the tiller more slowly; if the problem persists, raise the tines slightly to till at a shallower depth. You may have to experiment to find the right combination of speed and depth.

The Compost Pile: Free Fertilizer from Throwaways

Making a compost pile is somewhat like setting up a fertilizer factory in your backyard. The workers in the factory are millions of microorganisms—the bacteria and fungi that cause all organic materials to decay. In compost, transformations that take years on a forest floor can occur in four to six months. More specifically, organic waste from yard and kitchen is converted into humus, rich in nutrients and capable of improving the structure of the soil.

Compost bins hold the materials neatly and retain heat and moisture, which speed chemical changes. Such bins range from old-time earth pits to stall-like assemblies of lumber or concrete blocks. The simplest and easiest kind, shown below, is pig wire—heavy-gauge mesh with rectangular openings about 4 by 6 inches—on an open circle of metal fencing stakes. Many gardeners build two bins: one for compost in the process of decaying, one for storing the finished product. Make each bin 3 to 5 feet high and at least 4 feet wide, with an opening wide enough for a wheelbarrow. If possible, place the bins in a shady area to retard drying, and keep a hose handy for watering the contents.

The ingredients of a compost heap are usually determined by what is readily available. A nearby riding stable, producing a constant supply of manure and rotted straw, is an obvious boon. More common ingredients are fallen leaves and grass clippings from the yard; garden refuse, such as pulled weeds, hedge clippings and corn stalks; sawdust and wood shavings from a home workshop; wood ashes from a fireplace; and from the kitchen, vegetable scraps, crushed eggshells, coffee grounds and tea bags.

Although the variety of ingredients may be almost infinite, choosing the right amounts and mixing them together requires care. The microorganisms in compost work best on a diet richer in carbon than in nitrogen; a ratio of 30 parts of carbon to one of nitrogen is ideal. To obtain or approximate this ratio, mix materials relatively high in one element with those relatively high in the other. Woody, coarse materials tend to be high in carbon: Sawdust, for example, has a carbon-to-nitrogen ratio of 500 to 1; leaves, cornstalks and straw range between 40 and 80 to 1. Green or soft materials—grass clippings, vegetable scraps and manure—have ratios between 15 and 20 to 1; compared with the ideal 30-to-1 ratio, such materials are high in nitrogen.

In assembling the compost heap, work in layers of natural materials and soil. Make thick layers of coarse natural materials (about 6 inches of leaves, for example), thinner layers of light ones (about 3 inches of grass clippings, perhaps). A garden shredder, purchased or rented, reduces all composting materials to a single texture and speeds decomposition; if you use one, make all the layers 4 to 6 inches thick.

To provide food for the bacteria that break compost down and to add valuable minerals, top each layer of natural materials with a balanced commercial fertilizer or with manure; then, if your soil is too acid, add lime. Wet each layer with a garden hose and seal it with 2 inches of soil. Such soil sandwiches should be piled to the top of the bin; shape the topmost soil seal to a dishlike form to help collect rain water.

Most professional gardeners turn the pile with a spading fork every four weeks or so, a practice that speeds composting by incorporating air and by moving materials from the edges of the pile to the warm, brewing center. Even in the coldest weather, the chemistry of a compost pile should generate perceptible heat; the poet Robert Frost described the process as "the slow, smokeless burning of decay."

When ready for harvest, a compost heap is reduced in bulk by at least a third, and its ingredients are uniformly dark and flaky. Use compost generously: A 2-inch layer mixed deep into your soil twice a year is an ideal tonic.

Cover for a steep or rugged expanse. Sold by the flat, and easily divided and planted with a trowel, pachysandra is one of the hardiest of the 23 common evergreen ground covers that thrive in North America *(page 61)*. Its deeply toothed leaves grow in clusters and form a lush carpet 8 to 10 inches high, ideal for terrain too steep or rocky for a traditional grass lawn.

For many a homeowner, landscaping begins and ends with the lawn. Certainly, more effort is expended in seeding, mowing, watering, fertilizing, weeding and patching lawns than in all other landscaping activities combined. A peculiar mystique associated with attractive lawns inspires this effort. Part of the mystique has to do with the lawn itself: A velvety expanse of green is undeniably beautiful and has become as much a status symbol as a two-car garage or an outdoor swimming pool. Part has to do with the relation of the lawn to other plantings: Even the most mundane arrangements of shrubs, trees and flower beds take on new dimensions when displayed against the rich green of a well-tended lawn.

Lawns were not always so precious. The word "lawn" is derived from a Celtic term for a gladelike open space between wooded areas. Centuries ago, these natural lawns, sparsely covered with wild meadow grasses, were used as recreation areas where villagers played the games that would later become bowling, tennis and croquet. At that time, the only plants in house yards were those that could be used for food or for medicine.

Gradually, new species of hybridized grasses for home use evolved into today's wide assortment of durable, disease-resistant and uniformly toned lawn grasses. It is these breeds that make up the thick green blankets so many strive for and cherish, sometimes to the point of fencing in lawns and forbidding any traffic over them.

Actually, there is no need to pamper a properly maintained lawn. It is resilient enough to bounce back overnight from the occasional pounding of a lawn party or a volleyball game. But there is no escape from a continuous regimen of lawn upkeep throughout the growing season. Mowing and watering have become weekend—and, often, weekday—institutions; fertilizing, aerating, dethatching, weeding and reseeding, though performed less often, are essential if you want to turn an ordinary lawn into an outstanding one.

One way to break free of the burden of grass care is to plant something other than grass. Many lawns, especially those that have sloped or uneven surfaces, are made up of leafy ground covers, such as English ivy or Virginia creeper. Most of these plants require little more than periodic pruning, but they are comparatively fragile; unlike grass, they cannot take the pounding of human activity and traffic. A number of ground covers are earth-bound vines, many of which can be trained to grow vertically as readily as they do horizontally. This versatility can give an added dimension to a lawn in which vines not only cover the lawn area, but extend its borders skyward in walls of green that mute or even blot out the lines and colors of unattractive structures.

Painstaking Care for a Perfect Lawn

A lush, deep-green lawn rewards the homeowner who gives grass the special care it needs. But the reward does not come easily. Unless such tasks as mowing, fertilizing, watering and reseeding are painstakingly and correctly performed, the perfect lawn will elude even the best gardener.

Of these basic chores, mowing is by far the most time-consuming; in the spring a lawn may need mowing every week. Ideally, grass should be mowed to about two thirds of the height to which it has grown at mowing time; recommended mowed heights for the most common lawn grasses are given in the chart on page 54.

For the best appearance of a lawn cut a neat edge at the border: Most grasses can spread quickly into adjacent flower beds and unpaved walkways. Although tools called edgers can stop their progress temporarily, you may want to consider a permanent solution—a so-called mowing strip, usually consisting of a concrete or brick border. The strip not only halts the spread of grass but eases mowing at the lawn border by providing a grass-free path for the outer wheels of the mower.

In summer, when high heat and lower rainfall slow grass growth, you will mow your lawn less but water it more. Like mowing, watering calls for some self-restraint (extreme overwatering can be as damaging as drought) and for careful timing. Frequent light waterings end up inhibiting root growth, because the grass need not root deeply in quest of ground water; an occasional thorough watering—perhaps as seldom as once a week—is generally preferable. You can control the amount of water your lawn receives by using a sprinkler set for the correct intensity and area (pages 42-43), and you should monitor the depth to which the water penetrates (page 43).

Grass does not, of course, live by water alone. To replace soil nutrients, fertilizers should be added to a lawn three times during the growing season. The timing depends on the type of grass, as indicated in the chart on page 54. For northern grasses, such as bluegrass or fescue, make the first application in spring, the second and third within a month of each other in late summer and early fall. Feed southern grasses, such as Bermuda grass or zoysia, twice in spring, with a month between applications, then again in midsummer.

Lawn fertilizers come in powder, pellet and liquid form, with labels that rate the nitrogen, phosphorus and potassium content according to a three-number code. One common rating, 10-6-4, indicates that 10 per cent of the fertilizer bulk is nitrogen, 6 per cent phosphorus and 4 per cent potassium. The higher the rating, the higher the dose of nutrients; a fertilizer with a rating of 20-12-8 contains twice as much nutrient as the same amount of 10-6-4.

Consider these differences in nutrient values when comparing fertilizer prices. An average lawn needs 3 or 4 pounds of nitrogen per year for 1,000 square feet. The amount of fertilizer required for that area annually is between 30 and 40 pounds of 10-6-4, or from 15 to 20 pounds of doubly potent 20-12-8.

Most fertilizer formulations are balanced for normal feedings, with relatively large doses of nitrogen—roughly twice as much as either phosphorus or potassium. At least two times in each growing season, however, you should make a soil test (page 33) to be sure that your soil is not deficient in any of these three minerals; if it is deficient in one of them, use fertilizer with a higher proportion of that mineral. As part of the soil test, measure the soil's pH, or acidity. Most grasses prefer a pH between 6 and 6.5; if necessary, adjust the pH with appropriate chemicals (page 32), using a spreader.

With age even a lawn pampered by water and fertilizer can deteriorate. The ground beneath it may become so compacted by heavy traffic that grass roots cannot penetrate the hardened soil; at its worst, wear and tear can leave bare spots, which must be reseeded (page 47). A second common problem of aging is thatch, a layer of dead grass and weeds that can strangle new growth by preventing fresh seedlings from germinating.

Compaction and thatch are corrected with specialized lawn tools. An aerator (pages 11 and 45), which extracts small plugs of earth to loosen compacted soil, may be needed for heavily used backyards or play areas as often as every two years. A layer of thatch more than ¾ inch thick should be stripped off with a dethatching rake or a mechanical dethatcher (pages 10 and 46); both devices cut slits through the tightly woven barrier so it can easily be raked away.

Safety Tips for Mowers

The blades of rotary lawn mowers are a major cause of home accidents in the United States. Whirling at speeds up to 200 miles per hour, such a blade can slice through a shoe or finger as easily as it cuts a blade of grass, and hurl stones and metal objects at high velocity. When using a rotary mower, therefore, observe these basic precautions:
□ Before operating the mower for the first time, practice using the on-off controls, so that you can stop the machine quickly in an emergency.
□ Before each mowing, remove stones, branches, wires and rubbish from the lawn. Note and plan to avoid sprinkler heads and other fixed obstacles.
□ Unless your mower is equipped with a lever that enables you to adjust the height of the blade while the mower is running, make all cutting-height adjustments before starting the engine.
□ Before removing grass from the discharge chute of a power mower, turn off the engine and allow the blade to come to a stop.
□ When using a walking mower on a hill, mow across the slope, not up and down it, to prevent your feet from slipping underneath the mower. Riding mowers, on the other hand, are safer and more stable when they are run up and down a slope.

A Mower for Every Task

A reel mower. The scissoring action of reel blades against a fixed metal bed knife makes a smooth cut, particularly on thin grasses such as bluegrass; reel mowers are less effective in trimming denser grasses such as zoysia. The blades need frequent sharpening and are easily damaged by twigs or pebbles. Manual models are traditional on American lawns, but the self-propelled power model shown here is preferable for lawns larger than ¼ acre.

Rotary mowers. The sickle action of a high-speed blade cuts a clean swath through any type of grass, even in relatively irregular ground. Rotary blades for a walking model (*below, right*) come in lengths from 18 to 32 inches; easily removable, the blade must be kept sharp with a steel file to avoid fraying or tearing the grass. For areas larger than ½ acre, a riding rotary mower (*left*) with a longer blade offers advantages of speed and convenience.

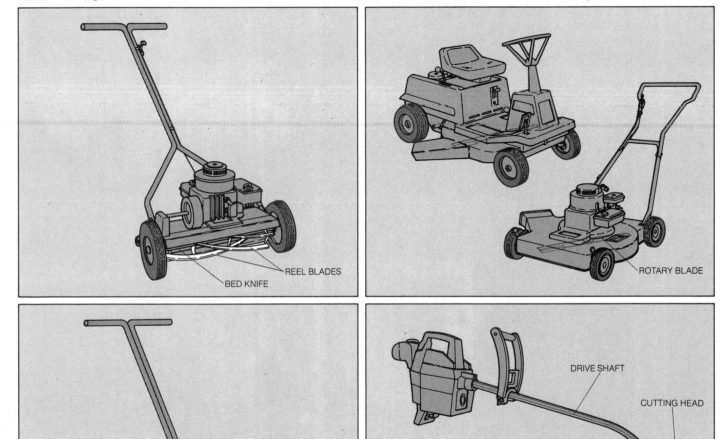

REEL BLADES
BED KNIFE

ROTARY BLADE

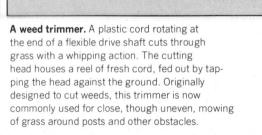

DRIVE SHAFT
CUTTING HEAD
PLASTIC CORD

A flail mower. Y-shaped blades swing loosely around a horizontal drum, threshing the grass with a rough cut that tends to fray grass tips. Because the blades give on contact with a hard object, a flail mower can be used safely on stony or rubbish-strewn areas.

A weed trimmer. A plastic cord rotating at the end of a flexible drive shaft cuts through grass with a whipping action. The cutting head houses a reel of fresh cord, fed out by tapping the head against the ground. Originally designed to cut weeds, this trimmer is now commonly used for close, though uneven, mowing of grass around posts and other obstacles.

How to Mow
a Lawn

Setting the blade height. With the engine off, tip the mower back and, reaching underneath it with a ruler, measure the distance from the blade to the bottom edge of the deck. Transfer this measurement to the outside of the deck with a pencil, then set the mower upright and measure from the mark to the ground to determine the present blade height.

If your mower is equipped with height-adjustment levers *(right)*, move the lever on each wheel to raise or lower the deck to the correct height—normally about 1 to 2 inches. On some models the height is adjusted by moving the wheel bolts to lower or higher holes. Riding mowers and some rotary models have a height lever that enables the operator to avoid obstacles by raising the blade while the mower is in motion.

Following the mowing patterns. On flat ground, start at the center of the lawn and mow in a pattern of expanding rectangles, making gradual turns at each end of the lawn and overlapping each swath by one third the width of the mower. To prevent ruts and striping, perform the next mowing at a 90° angle to this pattern; continue to alternate the direction of the cuts for each successive mowing.

When using a walking mower on a slope, begin at the lowest edge, mow across the slope in parallel lines up the hillside, lapping each cut by one third the width of the mower *(inset)*. With a riding mower, mow up and down the slope.

DECK

HEIGHT-ADJUSTMENT LEVERS

Trimming around obstacles. Use a weed trimmer to cut grass around posts or stones and beneath low-hanging branches or fencing, where a wheeled mower will not reach. Hold the cutting head parallel to the ground, an inch or so above the soil, and swing the cutter back and forth in smooth passes, working closer and closer to the obstacle until the level of the grass is even with the surrounding turf.

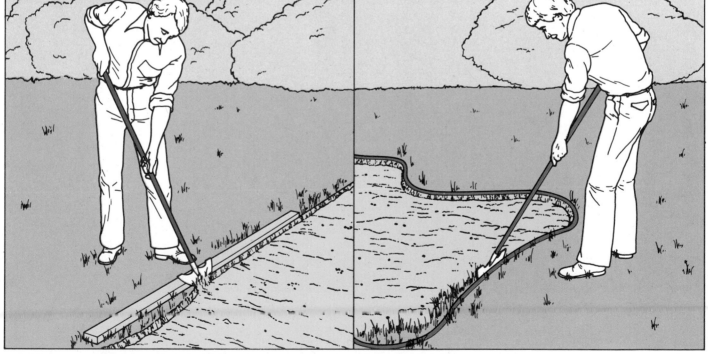

Edging. To cut a straight edge at the border of a path or flower bed, use a straight board as a guide for a half-moon edging hoe. Hold the hoe across the board at a slight angle and force the blade 2 to 3 inches into the earth along the board, slicing away about an inch of turf *(above, left)*. To produce a curved edge, lay a hose along the border and use it in the same way *(right)*, taking special care to keep the blade of the hoe flat against the hose at all times.

Choosing the Right Sprinkler

In some cool, wet regions, regular rainfall makes lawn watering superfluous, but most lawns need artificial soaking. A lack of water soon makes itself apparent in changes of texture and color: The grass loses its springy resilience and turns grayish, then almost blue. Eventually, the blades turn brown at the tips; soon afterward, they may wither and die. Grass rescued early in the gray stage by a thorough dousing from a sprinkler will revive in a few hours; brown blades may take weeks to reestablish themselves—and may be beyond saving.

Each of the sprinklers shown on these pages is designed to water an area of a specific size and shape. Choose the right sprinkler for your yard, then monitor its performance (opposite, bottom) to keep from either wasting water or giving the grass insufficient water.

Almost all grasses send roots to at least 6 inches below the surface of the soil.

Watering to a level below 6 inches, which encourages healthy root growth and vigorous turf, is best accomplished with a thorough weekly soaking rather than shallow daily sprinklings. But to a certain extent, the type of soil also governs watering practices. Water filters quickly through sandy soil, so that lighter but more frequent waterings may be needed. Dense, clayey soils require an especially slow, fine misting to allow time for water to seep in.

The best time of day for watering is the early morning; this soaks the ground soon enough to prevent the grass from wilting during the hottest part of the day. Watering in the evening can leave the blades damp and susceptible to fungus. Midday watering is worst of all: It is inefficient, because too much water evaporates, and it is dangerous to the grass, because water on grass blades can focus the sun's rays and burn the plants.

An Array of Sprinkling Patterns

An oscillating sprinkler. Driven by water pressure from a garden hose, an oscillating sprinkler provides an even dousing of a rectangular area of grass. The curved crosspiece swings back and forth through all or part of the arc indicated by arrows; controls at the base of the crosspiece set the sprinkler to water all of the lawn, the center alone or either half (shaded areas, inset).

A turret sprinkler. Multiple turrets on the face of the sprinkler can be aimed to vary the length and width of a rectangular pattern of spray, from square to oblong (inset). As compared with an oscillator, a turret sprinkler provides a quick, heavy, somewhat uneven dousing.

TURRETS

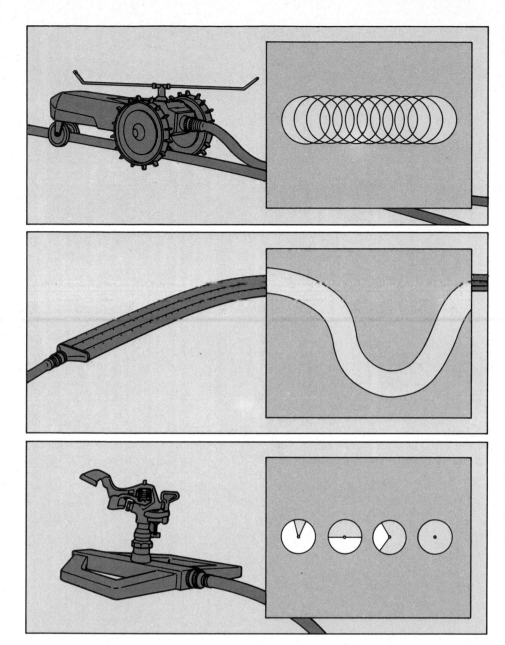

A traveling sprinkler. This self-propelled sprinkler is ideal for long, thin lawns. It follows the path of its own hose, even uphill, while the spinning nozzle soaks the grass in a spiral pattern *(inset)*. The traveling sprinkler shown here drags its hose behind it; other models reel in the slack hose as they move over the grass.

A perforated hose. Tiny holes along the top of a triple channel provide a fine soaking mist, excellent for clayey soils. The flexible hose can be laid to match the contours of an irregular plot *(inset)* or used with another hose section, linked by a Y joint, to cover wider areas. Other models come with double or single channels; a one channel hose, ideal for watering a border or a row of shrubs, is shown on page 86.

A pulsating sprinkler. The head of this sprinkler waters grass in a circular pattern that can be adjusted from a narrow wedge to a full circle *(inset)*. Constant side-to-side swings prevent water from pooling (a dose of moisture is absorbed by the grass before the nozzle delivers more) and spray can be varied from a short, fine burst to a long, heavy jet.

A Test for Penetration

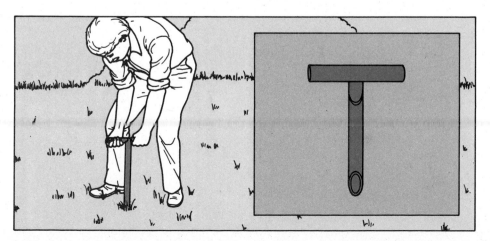

Boring with a core sampler. Soak the lawn for a half hour, then press and twist a core sampler— a hollow metal tube with a T handle *(inset)*— into the soil to a depth of at least 8 inches. Withdraw the tool and inspect the bottom of the soil sample within it. If the soil is dark with moisture, the watering was adequate; fill the hole with the soil of the sample, topping it with the removed sod. If the soil is dry, refill the hole, water for another half hour and take another sample; repeat this procedure until a sample is moist at the bottom. Note the total time needed to saturate the ground to the correct depth, and soak the lawn this long in future waterings.

Two Ways to Apply Fertilizer

Using a trough spreader. Standing at a corner of the lawn, set the spreader gauge, which controls the rate at which fertilizer falls from the trough, according to the instructions on the fertilizer package. Open the trough with the release lever and start walking immediately at an even, moderate pace along one end of the lawn. Close the trough as soon as you reach the far side, in order to avoid burning the grass with excess fertilizer. Turn the spreader around, open the trough and run a second row of fertilizer alongside the first, carefully positioning the spreader so that the two rows touch but do not overlap; a gap between rows will eventually leave dull streaks in the lawn. Run two similar rows at the opposite end of the lawn; then, running rows perpendicular to the end rows, fill in the remaining area *(inset)*.

Using a broadcast spreader. Push the spreader at an even pace that scatters the fertilizer in a row 6 to 8 feet wide; the speed of your pace determines the force of scattering and the width of the row. Work back and forth in wide parallel sweeps, overlapping the rows by about 1 foot and approaching corners and boundaries close enough to give them full coverage. Repeat the pattern at a right angle to the original rows *(inset)*.

END ROWS

END ROWS

RELEASE LEVER

SPREADER GAUGE

Breaking Up Compacted Soil

1 Aerating. Saturate the ground with a sprinkler a day in advance. Then, for a small lawn, thrust a 3- or 4-tined aerating fork *(below, left)* into the ground at 6-inch intervals, driving it to a depth of 2 inches in sandy soil, 4 inches in clayey soil. Work along one boundary, and then back and forth parallel to this line, leaving the extracted cores scattered on the ground. If the soil is so compacted that you cannot drive the aerating fork to the correct depth, make a shallower pass with the aerator, resoak the lawn and try again.

For large areas, use a self-propelled power aerator *(right)*. Roll the machine into position on the lawn, pull the starter cord and warm the engine with the clutch disengaged for three minutes. Release the front-wheel control lever, engage the clutch to start the corer drum, then adjust the throttle to maintain a slow, even speed. Guide the aerator in the pattern used for mowing *(page 40)*, but do not overlap the rows.

CLUTCH

THROTTLE

FRONT-WHEEL LEVER

2 Crumbling the cores. Tie a heavy cord to a 2-by-4-foot section of chain-link fencing and drag the mesh repeatedly over the lawn, reducing the extracted cores to spreadable soil. Use a grass rake to remove any other debris, such as stones and roots.

Spread a ½-inch layer of peat moss over the lawn. With the back of an iron rake, spread the moss and the soil from the cores over the yard, filling the core holes. Rake off any excess soil, then water the lawn thoroughly.

Cutting Through Layers of Thatch

Dethatching. For a small plot of grass, use a dethatching rake *(right, top)*. Holding the rake handle at a 30° angle to the ground, drag the rake across the lawn in parallel lines, exerting enough downward pressure to drive the teeth about ½ inch into the soil; take special care to avoid uprooting the grass or loosening the turf. Remove the thatch with a flexible grass rake.

For large areas, use a self-propelled power dethatcher *(bottom)*. Roll the dethatcher to the center of the lawn and start the engine with the clutch disengaged. Pull the height lever to lower the blades into the thatch, then turn the adjustment knob until the blades barely penetrate the soil. Engage the clutch, then run the machine over the lawn; follow the pattern used for mowing (page 40), but do not overlap the dethatching rows. Use a flexible grass rake to gather the loosened thatch, and mow the lawn to sever any sprigs that have been raised by the blades.

CLUTCH

ADJUSTMENT KNOB

BLADE-HEIGHT LEVER

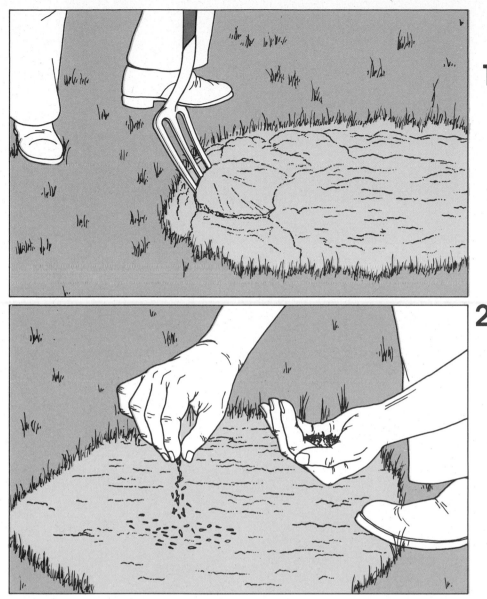

Reseeding a Bare Patch

1 Preparing the soil. Turn the soil in the plot with a spading fork, digging down 5 or 6 inches. Remove 3 inches of soil and work the remaining soil to break up clods. Dust the area lightly with lawn fertilizer and add a 3-inch layer of peat moss, then mix the soil, fertilizer and moss thoroughly with the spading fork.

Make the soil even with the surrounding earth by tamping it down with your foot. Your footprint should be no more than ½ inch deep in the soil mix; if necessary, adjust the soil level, either by removing mix or by adding more and tamping it down. Smooth the surface with the back of an iron rake.

2 Reseeding. Sprinkle seeds of grass about ⅛ inch apart over the patch, dropping the seeds from between your thumb and forefinger to avoid overseeding. Using an iron rake, work the seeds into the top ⅛ inch of soil mix, then tamp the soil lightly with the back of a hoe. Cover the patch with a very thin layer of straw— half the soil should show through—and spray the soil with a light mist from a garden hose.

When All Else Fails: Artificial Turf

Many a prospective lawn site harbors a fatal flaw. A layer of subterranean stone, for example, can defy all attempts at seeding, or the turf beside a driveway may be permanently defoliated by deicing salts used in winter. Sometimes homeowners consciously render a site unusable. Weary of seeding and feeding, they may resort to a concrete paving that solves the problem for good—then find that they miss the green of their banished grass.

In such cases, an artificial turf—actually outdoor carpet made of plastic— can provide a sense of grass without the endless need for care. The ersatz product is expensive and lacks the cool, lush feel of grass, but it is water-, fade- and rot-resistant, and it gives years of maintenance-free ground cover.

If the artificial expedient appeals to you, choose a pile height and density suited to the traffic in your yard. A light, 12- to 16-ounce density, with a low, ⅛-inch pile height will do for lightly used sites. Play areas and heavily traveled paths need a sturdier cover and a more expensive density (up to 40 ounces), with a pile from ½ to ¾ inch high.

Artificial-turf carpet can be installed on any smooth, dry base of concrete or asphalt. Clean the surface carefully and fill any cracks wider than ⅛ inch with a cement-based grout. Be sure to bond the carpet to its base with the specific waterproof adhesive recommended by the manufacturer: The adhesive must be compatible with the foam, vinyl or rubber backing of the carpet.

Fighting Weeds by Hand and Herbicide

The best defense against an invasion of lawn weeds is the lawn itself: A dense carpet of healthy turf can prevent weeds from gaining a toehold, by depriving them of the sunlight they need to germinate and multiply. But even in the best-kept lawn, some weeds are inevitable. When they do arise, they must be removed by hand or killed by chemicals.

Botanists distinguish between grassy and broad-leaved weeds, and the two types call for different chemical treatments. Grassy weeds, including the infamous crab grass, can be caught early with a so-called preemergent weed killer, which destroys the germinating plants just as they emerge; established weeds must be treated with a postemergent type, which attacks the growing plant. Broad-leaved weeds—plantain and dandelion, for example—are treated with chemical hormones, such as 2,4-D or glysophate, which accelerate growth to a point where the burgeoning weeds literally starve themselves to death.

All of these chemicals must be used with caution. They can attack trees and shrubs that are accidentally treated, and the grassy-weed chemicals also present a hazard to some turf grasses; check the package label to be sure that the one you choose is safe for the grasses in your lawn, particularly if it is freshly sown.

To protect yourself and nearby plants, spray only on windless days. If the winds in your locality are high and constant or if the layout of your plantings makes the risk of contamination unavoidable, use a weeder bar or roller (opposite), impregnated with chemicals; it can kill weeds over a large area without spraying. Your best protection, however, is to reduce the use of chemicals by stopping a weed invasion before it spreads. The spot treatments shown on this page, applied in spring before weeds have established a toehold, can eliminate the need for broader coverage later on.

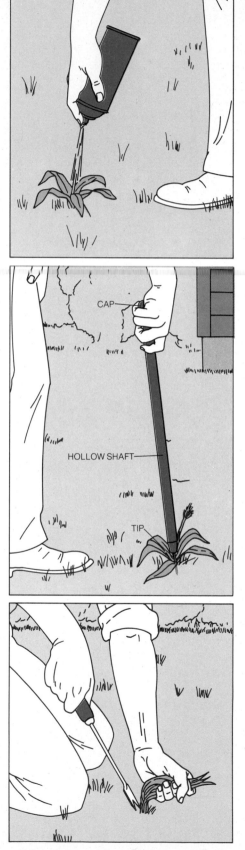

Spot Treatments That Catch Weeds Early

An aerosol herbicide. Hold the aerosol can 8 to 12 inches above the weed, and spray a one-second burst onto the center of the plant, coating the leaves and main stem. Allow the weed about two weeks to shrivel and die, then remove it and reseed (page 47) or sprig (page 52) the bare spot.

A weed wand. Using a funnel, fill the hollow shaft of the wand with weed killer, then cap the wand and press the retractable tip down into the center of the weed, close to the root. Use the herbicide sparingly; a two- or three-second application is usually enough to kill a weed.

A weeding fork. Grasp all of the weed's runners or leaves in one hand; with the other, drive a weeding fork 3 or 4 inches into the earth alongside the main root. Levering the fork back and forth in the surrounding soil to work the roots free, pull up lightly on the bunched leaves until you can remove the weed with all its roots intact. It may be necessary to dig the fork all the way around an unusually stubborn weed; you must remove the weed without tearing its leaves or breaking its roots.

Treating a Large Area

Using a pressurized sprayer. Along one end of the weed-infested area, mark off a 1-yard strip with a pair of staked parallel strings. Build up pressure in the sprayer with a few strokes of the hand pump, then spray the area between the strings, holding the wand about 12 inches above the grass and moving it quickly and steadily for a light, even coverage. Next, move one of the strings to mark off an adjoining strip, and treat this strip in the same way. Repeat this procedure until you have sprayed the entire area.

Using a garden-hose sprayer. With string and stakes, mark off a 200-square-foot area; set a conspicuous marker, such as a grass rake, at the middle of the area. Fill the sprayer jar with weed killer or with the mixture of weed killer and water specified in the label instructions; then screw the sprayer nozzle onto a garden hose and attach the jar to the nozzle. Open the hose valve and start the sprayer by covering the air-siphon hole or by depressing the trigger lever, depending on your model. Spray the area with a light, even coat, adjusting your movement and the force of the spray so that the jar is half empty when you reach the halfway marker.

JAR

SPRAYER NOZZLE

Weeding with a wax bar. Mow the lawn, then slowly pull the wax bar over the infested area in parallel sweeps; pull the bar cord at a low angle to get at patches of lawn that lie under low, overhanging trees and shrubs, which would be damaged by a spray. Finally, water the lawn thoroughly to work the weed killer into the soil.

Four Foolproof Ways to Start a New Lawn

To establish a lawn on an empty lot or to renovate an old lawn terminally choked with weeds, you must build a lawn from scratch. The job is not complicated, but it does involve heavy preliminary work. Before planting can begin, the yard must be cleared. The ground must be cultivated to a depth of about 5 or 6 inches. Then, depending on the results of soil tests, it may have to be further improved with fertilizers and conditioners (*page 54*). Finally, the plot must be raked and rolled smooth. Only then is the soil ready to support a stand of new grass.

The type of grass you should choose for your plot depends largely upon the climate of your region. No turf grass is suitable everywhere; many will not survive extremes of heat or cold, and some tolerate dry climates better than others do. But certain rules of thumb apply. So-called cool-season grasses, such as bluegrass and fescue, are well adapted for northern climates. Such grasses grow slightly in spring, languish in the warm months of a relatively short summer and thrive in a cool, wet autumn. Ideally, they should be planted in late summer to take advantage of the autumn growing season, but they can also be sown on frozen ground in early spring, before the first mild weather.

Warm-season grasses, such as Bermuda, zoysia or St. Augustine, have the opposite schedule, flourishing in the heat of a long summer and going dormant in cool months. Plant them in spring or early summer, when daytime temperatures are regularly above 70° F. For lawns with a combination of sunny and shaded areas or in climates with wide variations of temperature, a mixture of several grass types gives the best results. Mixtures are sold with the percentage of each grass type listed on the package, so that you can choose the mix that best suits your special conditions of light and climate.

With the soil bed prepared and the grass type chosen, you have a choice of four ways to plant the lawn, based on seed, sprigs, plugs or sod. Direct seeding is the least expensive method but also the slowest. Sprigs and plugs, listed here in increasing order of expense, are closely related: The first consists of grass stems with roots and blades attached; the second of small pieces of sod. Sodding, in which rectangular pieces of live turf are set on bare ground, is the quickest of all four methods—and the most expensive.

If you choose to seed a lawn, follow the seeding density given on the label of the grass mixture or in the chart on page 54, and spread the seed evenly over the area by hand or with a mechanical spreader. Do not try to speed growth by using more than the recommended quantity of seed; the seedlings will essentially rob one another of nutrients and will eventually produce an unhealthy-looking lawn. Once they are in the ground, seeds need constant moisture to germinate; water the lawn daily, or even every few hours in extreme heat. Leave the grass untouched until it is 3 inches high, then mow it to promote spreading.

Most warm-season grasses and all sterile hybrids (which produce no seeds) are planted by sprigging or plugging. Coverage is slow because the seedlings must send out new shoots to fill the gaps left between them in planting; but in the meantime the new lawn is somewhat less fragile than a lawn grown from seed. Nurseries sell flats of plugs and either flats or packages of sprigs, which must be peeled apart. Sprigs are simply set into shallow furrows scratched into the earth with a hoe blade. For plugging, you will need a plugging tool (*page 52*) fitted for the thickness of your plugs; the nursery that sells you the plugs will usually be able to rent you the tool.

For those who want the instant gratification of a ready-made, almost prefabricated lawn, sodding is ideal. Mats of sod are ready for use immediately, but laying them down calls for careful leveling of the bed and much heavy lifting of the rolls. You will get the best results if you lay the sod within 36 hours after delivery, while it is still fresh and moist. Have the plot leveled before the delivery date; keep the soil bed moist but not muddy while laying the rolls, to ensure good contact with the soil—and, obviously, do not order more sod than you can lay within 36 hours.

A New Lawn from Seed

1 **Firming the soil.** After tilling and conditioning the soil, push a lawn roller, empty of water, over the entire area. Roll the area first in parallel strips, then go over it again at a right angle (*inset*). If necessary, continue to firm and compact the soil until your feet barely leave an indentation; if the soil remains soft, fill the roller half full of water to add weight.

Smooth and spread the soil with an iron rake. Hold the rake at a 20° to 30° angle to avoid gouging the soil, and work the tines back and forth across the surface, pulling out and discarding any stones, rubbish or weeds. Finally, roll the soil once again to firm the surface.

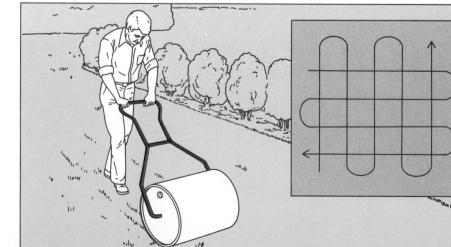

2 Smoothing the bed. Weight a ladder with a heavy plank and a pair of concrete blocks, tie the ends of a rope to one of the uprights and drag the ladder over the soil to slice off protruding mounds and fill depressions. Every 10 feet, set a carpenter's level across the ladder to check the slope of the bed. This slope should run slightly downward from the house, so that it will channel water away from the foundation walls; if necessary, regrade the bed (page 25) to adjust the slope. Finally, use an iron rake to roughen the soil lightly to a depth of ½ inch.

3 Sowing seed by hand. Measure out the correct quantity of seed for the entire area (chart, page 54), then divide the seed into two equal portions. Walk slowly over the plot in parallel lines, scattering seed from your open fist in 5-foot arcs until you have sown the entire area once with half the seed; then sow the area again with the other half of the seed, walking in rows at right angles to the first direction. Finally, rake the area once to a depth of ⅛ inch with a flexible grass rake to mix the seed into the soil.

In an alternative method, the seed can be sown with a mechanical spreader of the type shown on page 44. Follow the same sowing pattern, and be sure to rake the seed into the soil at the end of the job.

4 Mulching and watering. With a pitchfork, scatter a ½-inch layer of clean straw over the seedbed, covering the ground lightly so that half the soil can be seen beneath the straw. Water the bed with a gentle mist just long enough to soak the soil without forming puddles or rivulets. Until the seeds germinate, keep the soil constantly dark with moisture; then reduce the watering frequency to once a day until the seedlings are up through the straw. Do not mow or walk on the new grass until it is 3 inches high; at that point, either rake the mulch off or simply leave it to decompose into the soil.

Planting with Sprigs

1 Furrowing the soil. After preparing and leveling the soil (pages 50-51, Steps 1 and 2), soak the bed with water. Let the water seep in for 24 hours; then, with the corner of a garden-hoe blade, cut a series of straight furrows 3 to 4 inches deep and 6 to 12 inches apart. Rows of sprigs planted 6 inches apart usually form a full lawn within 6 months; rows set 12 inches apart take about 12 months.

2 Setting the sprigs. At 6- to 12-inch intervals, place the sprigs in the furrows, slanting them upward from the bottom of a furrow to the top of one side. Pack soil gently around the roots with your hands, leaving some blades of each sprig protruding above the ground. Smooth the soil and level it around the sprigs.

When you have planted all of the sprigs, follow the same watering procedure as for a bed sown with seed (page 51, Step 4).

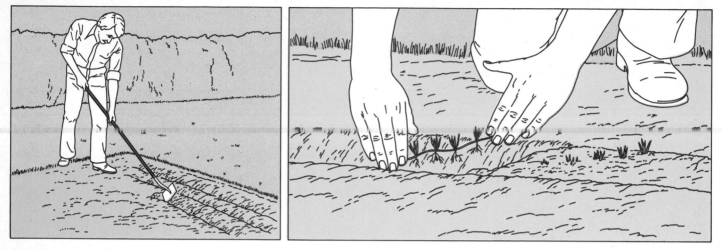

Planting with Plugs

1 Cutting holes for planting. Prepare the soil bed (pages 50-51, Steps 1 and 2), soak it thoroughly and let the water seep in for 24 hours, then make holes for the plugs, spaced 6 to 12 inches apart. To make each hole, step down on the foot bar of a plugging tool until the bar touches the ground; lift the tool straight up, extracting a core of soil, and push or tap the core out onto the ground. Plugs set 6 inches apart will spread to cover the lawn in 6 months; set 12 inches apart, they will take 12 months.

2 Planting the plugs. Fill the holes with water, allow the water to drain completely, then insert a plug in each hole. The bottom of the grass blades should be ¼ inch above the soil surrounding the plug; if necessary, pull the plug out of the planting hole and add or remove a small amount of soil with a gardening trowel to set the plug at the correct level.

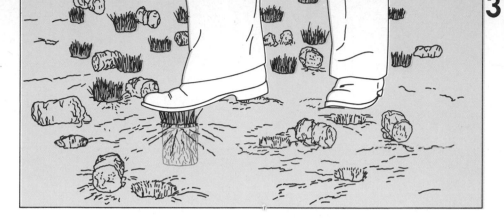

3 Tamping the soil. With the ball of your foot, step gently on each plug to bring it even with the surrounding soil and force its roots into solid contact with the bottom of the planting hole. Smooth the ground between plugs with a grass rake, spreading the dirt from the extracted soil cores and leveling out footprints. Follow the watering procedures for a bed sown with seed (*page 51, Step 4*).

An Instant Lawn from Rolls of Sod

1 Laying the sod. After preparing the bed (*pages 50-51, Steps 1 and 2*), roughen the surface slightly with an iron rake and wet the soil thoroughly. Unroll the sod gently to avoid breaking off corners and edges, and lay the first course as flat as possible along a straight pavement or a staked string to provide a straight edge. For later courses, kneel on a piece of plywood or planking laid across the new sod, to avoid creating depressions and raising the edges of sections. Butt the sod rolls as tightly as possible against each other, staggering the ends in an ordinary bricklaying pattern. If a laid roll feels uneven, roll it up and relevel the ground beneath it. Finally, fill any gaps between sections, cutting small pieces from a spare roll with a sharp knife or the edge of a trowel.

2 Establishing root contact. Tamp the sod with a tamping tool or with a board and rubber mallet, pressing the sod firmly against the soil bed; alternatively, roll the turf with an empty lawn roller (*page 50*). If, by either method, you inadvertently lift the edges of a sod section, take special care to tamp them down.

Water the sod every day for two weeks or longer, until the sod roots in the soil. To determine whether the sod has rooted, try to lift a small piece of sod by the grass blades; if the sod has rooted, the blades will tear.

Choosing a Grass for Your Lawn

Grass type	Growing areas	Recommended soil pH	Planting method	Seeding density (lbs./1,000 sq. ft.)	Planting season	Mowing height (inches)	Characteristics and maintenance
Northern grasses							
Bentgrass; colonial, creeping, red top, velvet (*Agrostis*)	3	5.3 to 7.5	seed, sprig, sod	1	fall	$\frac{3}{4}$	Thick, fine texture; shiny green. Grows in cool, humid climates. Needs constant maintenance. Water frequently, fertilize every month; dethatch yearly.
Bluegrass; Canada, Kentucky, roughstalk (*Poa*)	1,4,6	6.0 to 7.5	seed, sod	2-4	fall, early spring	2-2½	Dense, rich green, fine-textured turf. Drought-resistant and semidormant in warm weather.
Carpet grass (*Axonopus*)	3	4.7 to 7.0	seed, sprig, plug, sod	4-5	spring, early summer	1-2	Rugged, though spotty, light green turf. Survives with little maintenance in acidic, sandy and poorly drained soil and in wet locations.
Fescue; red, tall (*Festuca*)	1,2,4-6	5.3 to 7.5	seed, sod	4-8	fall, early spring	2-3	Tough, medium-textured turf. Forms clumps if too sparsely sown. Very low maintenance.
Rye grass; annual, Italian, perennial (*Lolium*)	2,3,5	5.5 to 8.0	seed, sod	5	late fall	2	Fast-growing, light green annual; good for overseeding Southern grasses before winter.
Wheat grass; crested, western (*Agropyron*)	4,5	6.0 to 8.5	seed, sod	1-2	fall, early spring	2-2½	Bluish green bunches; dormant in summer and tolerant of drought. Avoid overwatering and overfertilizing.
Southern grasses							
Bahia grass (*Paspalum*)	3	5.0 to 6.5	seed, sod	4-6	spring	2½-3	Light green, extremely coarse, drought-resistant.
Bermuda grass (*Cynodon*)	2,3,5	5.2 to 7.0	seed, sprig, plug, sod	2-3	late spring, summer	½-1½	Dense, lush, quick-spreading. Dark green to bluish, depending on hybrid. Dethatch each spring.
Blue grama grass (*Bouteloua*)	4,5	6.0 to 8.5	seed, sod	1-2	early spring	2-2½	Drought-resistant, small, grayish leaves, which form low tufts.
Buffalo grass (*Buechloe*)	4,5	6.0 to 8.5	seed, plug, sod	1-1½	fall, early spring	2-2½	Rugged, slow-growing, grayish blades, which make a very smooth-textured lawn.
Centipede grass (*Eremochloa*)	2,3,5	4.0 to 6.0	seed, sprig, plug, sod	⅛-¼	spring, early fall	2	Slow, low-growing, low-maintenance grass with yellowish, coarse leaves.
St. Augustine grass (*Stenotaphrum*)	2,3,5	6.0 to 7.0	sprig, plug, sod	—	spring	1-2	Coarse, dense, low-growing, bluish turf. Dethatch yearly.
Zoysia (Latin genus) Also called Manila, Mascarene, Japanese, Korean lawn grass	1-3,5,6	5.5 to 7.0	sprig, plug, sod	—	spring	½-1½	Dense, slow-growing turf, ranging from coarse grayish to fine moss green. Needs constant watering and fertilizing.

Common grass types. Use this chart to find a grass to suit your tastes, soil and climate. Grasses are divided into Northern and Southern types, and most are listed by their common English names, followed by their Latin botanical names. Across the top, column headings define the needs of each variety: the area or areas of North America in which each grass grows best, keyed to the map opposite; the best soil pH; the variety of practical planting methods, potentially including seeding, sodding, sprigging and plugging; the pounds of seed needed to sow an area of 1,000 square feet; the preferred planting seasons; and the ideal mowing height. The column at far right describes grass characteristics and maintenance needs; use this information to match a specific grass to your landscaping scheme and soil.

A Map of Grass Zones

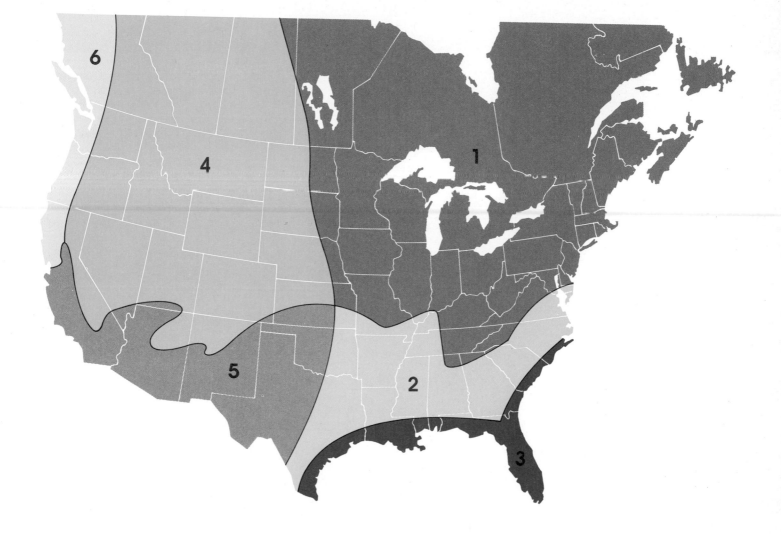

Different zones for different grasses. Each of the six regions outlined on the map above is particularly favorable for some of the common grasses listed in the chart opposite. The zones are based upon three environmental factors that are critical to grass health: minimum winter and maximum summer temperatures, annual rainfall, and acidity or alkalinity of soil. Temperature is the most obvious criterion: Northern grasses generally do well in Zones 1, 4 and 6; Southern grasses prefer Zones 2, 3 and 5. But Eastern and Western zones are also divided, partly because Eastern soils tend to be more acid than Western soils and partly because, on the whole, the East receives greater amounts of rainfall than does the West.

Weaving Diversified Carpets of Ground Covers

The low, rambling plants called ground covers, which grow in thick beds or mats, offer attractive alternatives to grasses in a variety of situations. On hillsides, ground covers check soil erosion and eliminate the troublesome—and risky—job of mowing on a slope. Many flourish in the shade and make hardy plantings for sunless areas that might otherwise be empty of greenery. And their diversity of color, foliage and flowers provides decorative notes that can break up the monotony of open spaces or form a transition between low grasses and tall shrubs.

Literally hundreds of plants can be used as ground covers. They range in size from dainty, 3-inch baby's tears to spindly, 2-foot-tall Scotch heather, and in color from the deep green of English ivy to the bright yellow blossoms of moneywort. The evergreens, such as bearberry, juniper and sand strawberry, keep a yard verdant all year long; deciduous plants, such as lily of the valley and woodruff, turn brown during the winter. Some herbaceous ground covers, such as thyme, are prized for their fragrance. And certain fast-growing vines—Virginia creeper and periwinkle, for example—can be trained to flourish flat on the ground.

Choosing ground covers is not a matter of taste alone. The chart on page 61 lists some of the popular varieties and provides information on their special requirements of soil and climate; in addition, you should consult your nursery about the varieties that are most appropriate for your locality. Before purchasing the plants, calculate exactly how many you will need: As a general rule, two to three such plants will cover a square foot of soil.

Some ground covers, such as evergreen candytuft and moss sandwort, can be grown from seed. Most, however, are sold as immature plants; they come assembled in groups of about 50 and planted in a rooting medium in a flat (below)—a shallow, plastic tray measuring about 12 by 15 inches and pierced with drainage holes.

To help keep weeds at bay, mulch the ground with a layer of shredded pine bark before you begin planting seeds or transferring plants from flats to the ground. (Even with such protection, the ground covers will have to be weeded—as often as every few days during the first year or so.) The mulch should be spread before planting because it is much easier and safer to dig holes in the ground through mulch than it is to distribute the bark around the delicate young plants.

Once the plants are out of their flats, plant them quickly so that their roots will not dry out. Experienced gardeners use an economical three-step troweling technique (opposite, top) to get the plants into the ground in the least amount of time. The young plants will need lots of water—a good drenching with a garden hose every other day for the first month.

After they have become well established, ground covers may run rampant. If they are not kept in check with judicious pruning, they will encroach on lawns and take over adjacent flower gardens. Such vigorous growth, however, represents an opportunity as well as a disadvantage: You can easily propagate new plants by either dividing or taking cuttings from established ones (pages 58-59).

Growing new ground-cover beds from old has other advantages than helping to control unwanted sprawl: It is less costly than buying extra plants from a nursery and assures a uniform appearance from bed to bed. New plants can never exactly match established ones in color or shape, but plants grown by division or cutting will display characteristics identical to those of their parents.

Getting Tiny Plants Off to a Good Start

1 **Separating the plants.** Work both hands under the rooting medium and lift the entire rectangle of packed medium out of the flat in one piece. Then separate the plants with your fingers, taking care not to injure the roots.

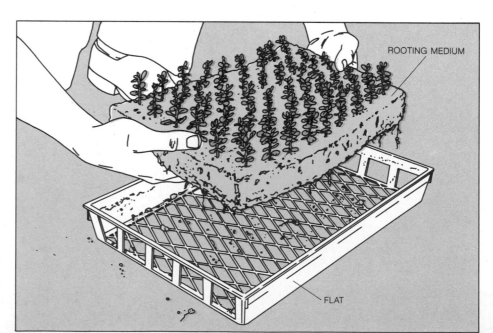

ROOTING MEDIUM

FLAT

2 Setting the plants. Working quickly, set the plants into the soil by a three-step procedure. First, prepare a planting hole: Push a trowel down through the mulch and into the soil, then pull the trowel toward you, cutting a small pocket in the ground (*below, left*). Second, put the plant in place: Holding the soil back with the trowel, set a plant in the pocket, with about ¼ inch of its stem below ground level (*center*). Finally, use the trowel to push the displaced soil back into the pocket (*right*), taking care not to dislodge or bruise the plant.

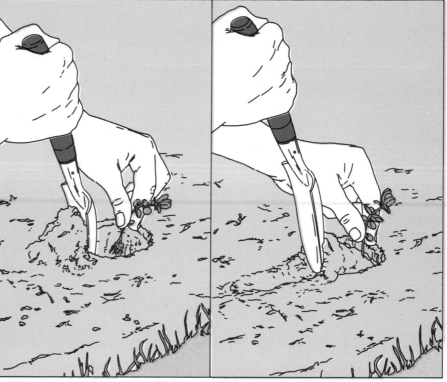

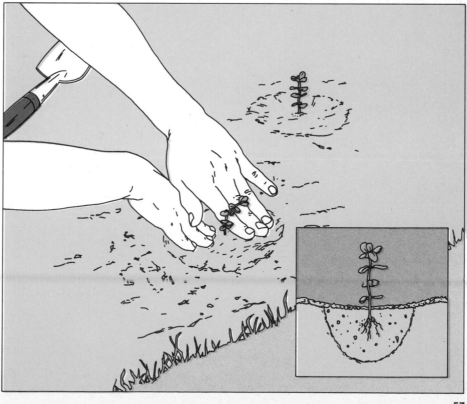

3 Tamping down the soil. Smooth out the soil and mulch with your fingers, patting the mulch down around the stem to form a slight depression that will catch and hold moisture (*inset*). Set in the remaining plants, and water them for at least half an hour with a lawn sprinkler or with a hose set for a fine mist. Continue to water the new plants every other day for the next month.

Multiplying by Dividing or Cutting

Ground covers can be propagated by three methods: layering, cutting and division. Layering, in which a branch is made to root in the soil without being cut from the parent plant, is used more often for shrubs than for ground covers. However, some woody ground covers, such as winter creeper, respond well to layering; if you choose this method for an appropriate plant, follow the instructions on page 93.

In propagation by cutting, a piece is removed from the upper part of a well-established plant at least a year old, and placed in a spot where it can sprout roots of its own. Plants with succulent, non-woody stems, such as bearberry and periwinkle, grow well from cuttings.

Ideal parent plants for cuttings have crisp stems that snap off cleanly when bent sharply. Each cutting should contain three to five nodes—small bumps along the stems, marking locations where new roots will emerge. To encourage rapid, healthy root growth, the stems are dipped in a synthetic, powdered plant hormone, available from nurseries or garden-supply outlets, then planted in flats filled with a rooting medium such as a combination of sand and peat moss in equal parts. Covered with sheets of glass or plastic, the flats become miniature greenhouses, protecting young plants until they can survive outdoors.

Ground covers with thick root masses —woodruff, mondo grass and lily of the valley, for example—respond best to division. Large clumps of established plants, each containing a dozen or more stems, are uprooted, then individual rooted stems are separated and planted elsewhere. Divided plants do not require babying, as cuttings do, but they have one requirement in common: Like newly purchased plants, both must be watered for half an hour every other day for a month.

The time of year to propagate new plants depends partly on the type of plant, partly on climate. Check with the nursery that supplied the original plants to find out the best time for your plants and locality.

Propagation by Cutting

1 **Obtaining a cutting.** Remove a 3- to 6-inch length from a parent-plant stem or an entire short stem, then cut through the removed stem with a small sharp knife, making a clean, sharply angled incision slightly below the nodes. This will expose the maximum area of the stem's interior to the nourishing rooting medium.

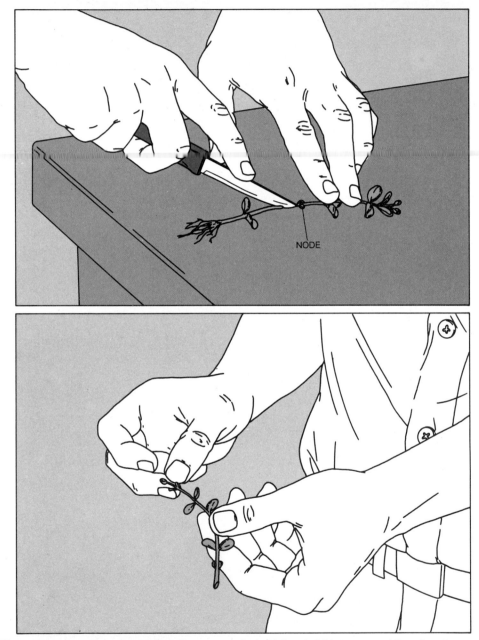

2 **Preparing the cutting for planting.** First, pinch off from the stem any flowers or seed heads; if allowed to remain, they would divert nutrients away from the roots that will form on the cutting. Also be certain that you trim away the leaves from any section of the stem that is going to be placed under the ground; buried foliage is liable to rot, providing a breeding ground for bacteria.

Allow the cut end of the stem to dry out slightly; if the leaves begin to wilt, place them on a damp towel. Just before planting the cutting, dip its end into plant hormone powder.

3 Planting the cuttings. Fill a flat to about an inch from the top with moistened rooting medium. Then, using a small sharp stick or a pencil, poke holes in the medium just deep enough to cover two or three nodes on the stems of the cuttings. Set each cutting in a hole, tamp the rooting medium down around it, and water the entire flat thoroughly but gently. Cover the flat with a sheet of glass or clear plastic.

Keep the flat in a warm room and out of direct sunlight until the roots are firmly established. As a rule, the appearance of new leaves is a good indication that the cuttings are ready to be moved outdoors. Plant them in a prepared bed, exactly as you would set in new plants (*pages 56-57*).

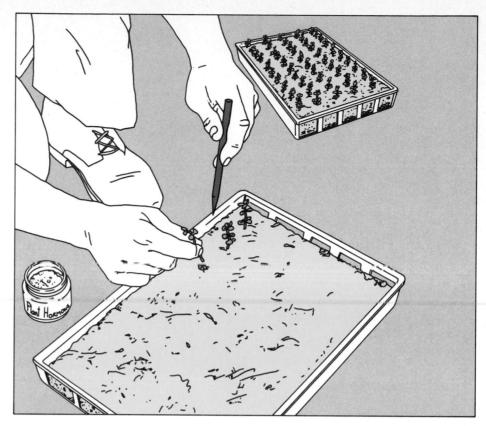

Propagation by Division

1 Uprooting the plants. Using a hand fork, dig out a clump of plants from a dense growth of ground covers. As you raise the clump, guide the roots away from the tines of the fork with your free hand. The clump should contain enough stems to produce about 10 new plants.

2 Separating the plants. Rinse away soil from the clump so that you can get a good view of the roots, then carefully pull the clump apart. Discard any wilted or yellowish-looking plants, return two or three of the plants to their original hole, and then set the rest of the plants in a new hole and water them thoroughly.

Coping With Slopes

A slope lends character and individuality to a home and its surroundings. A gentle grade, for example, can lead a visitor's eye to the front door; a rolling hill in the backyard can create a pleasant vista; a sharp embankment can separate the house from the street. But slopes also present some of the most challenging problems in landscaping.

Unplanted slopes exposed to heavy rains will almost certainly fall victim to soil erosion. Although grasses often grow well on slopes, maneuvering a lawn mower over hilly terrain is awkward and hazardous. Swift-growing ground covers, with deep roots to hold the soil and thick leaves to catch and disperse water, are often the ideal solution.

The first rule of growing ground covers on any slope is to position the plants in staggered rows, creating a diamond-shaped pattern that prevents water from washing straight down the hill in furrows. On moderate slopes of 30° or less, drive unpainted wooden sticks among the plants to hold the soil in place until the new roots have developed fully. Use foot-long dowels, unused paint stirrers, laths or the like, and drive them deep enough into the ground to set their tops below the tops of the mature plants; the only requirement is that the wood must be untreated so that undesirable chemicals do not get into the soil. The sticks can be left permanently in the ground, since they will soon be obscured by the plants.

On slopes steeper than 30°, use only the fastest-growing ground covers, such as periwinkle, and plant them very close together. Add an extra layer of mulch or a covering of coarse burlap netting to the ground before planting to help hold the soil until the roots are firmly established.

Very steep slopes may require terracing or even a retaining wall *(pages 27-31)*, and you can enhance the natural charm of a mortarless retaining wall by creating a rock garden in its crevices. A number of small, rambling plants, such as catmint, thrive in an environment of rooting medium packed in the cracks between the masonry.

Planting shoots and sticks. Position new plants or seedlings on a slope in staggered rows. Thrust foot-long, untreated wooden stakes into the ground among the plants, driving the sticks to a depth of about 8 inches and spacing them about 8 inches apart along the plant rows.

Finishing touches for a retaining wall. To prepare a stone wall as a host for plants, first loosely fill the cracks between the stones with garden soil. Using a long-handled wooden spoon, tamp the soil 1 to 2 inches into the crevices in the front of the wall and then stuff chunks of a rooting medium such as peat moss into the spaces *(inset)*. After poking holes in the rooting medium with your finger or with a small pointed stick, set the plants into the holes and tamp the rooting medium gently. Water the plants with a fine mist from a hand-held hose.

A Selection of Ground Covers

Plant	Zones	Special uses: Slopes	Rock gardens	Soil: Moist	Dry	Light: Partial shade	Full sun	Special traits: Flowers or fruits	Vine	Rapid growth	Easy maintenance	Height: Under 8 in.	8 to 16 in.	Over 16 in.	Foliage color: Green	Gray-green	Propagation: Cuttings	Division	Layering
EVERGREEN																			
Bearberry (ARCTOSTAPHYLOS UVA-URSI)	2-10	●			●		●			●		●		●					●
Candytuft, evergreen (IBERIS SEMPERVIRENS)	3-10					●	●				●	●			●		●	●	
Carmel creeper (CEANOTHUS GRISEUS HORIZONTALIS)	7-10	●				●	●						●	●	●				
Coyote brush (BACCHARIS PILULARIS)	8-10	●				●	●			●	●			●	●				
Daisy, trailing African (OSTEOPERMUM FRUTICOSUM)	9-10	●				●	●	●		●			●		●	●	●		
Dichondra (DICHONDRA REPENS)	9-10		●				●			●	●	●			●			●	
Geranium, strawberry (SAXIFRAGA STOLONIFERA)	8-10			●		●	●	●		●	●	●			●			●	●
Grape, dwarf holly (MAHONIA REPENS)	5-10	●		●			●	●		●			●		●			●	
Heath, spring (ERICA CARNEA)	5-10	●		●			●	●				●			●		●		
Heather, Scotch (CALLUNA VULGARIS)	4-10	●		●			●			●		●			●		●		
Ivy, English (HEDERA HELIX)	5-10	●	●	●					●	●	●	●			●				
Juniper, Wilton carpet (JUNIPERUS HORIZONTALIS WILTONII)	2-10	●		●		●				●	●				●	●			
Lily-turf, creeping (LIRIOPE SPICATA)	4-10						●			●		●			●			●	
Pachysandra, Japanese (PACHYSANDRA TERMINALIS)	4-9	●		●		●		●		●	●	●			●		●		
Periwinkle, common (VINCA MINOR)	4-10	●		●		●		●	●	●	●	●			●		●		
Plum, Green Carpet Natal (CARISSA GRANDIFLORA)	10		●				●					●			●				
Sandwort, moss (ARENARIA VERNA SATUREJA)	2-10	●		●			●	●			●	●			●			●	
Snow-in-summer (CERASTIUM TOMENTOSUM)	2-10		●			●	●	●		●	●	●				●	●	●	
Strawberry, sand (FRAGARIA CHILOENSIS)	8-10					●	●	●		●		●				●			
Thyme, wild (THYMUS SERPYLLUM)	3-10				●		●	●		●	●	●				●			
Thrift, common (ARMERIA MARITIMA)	2-10		●				●	●			●				●		●		
Yarrow, woolly (ACHILLEA TOMENTOSA)	2-10		●		●		●	●		●	●	●			●	●	●	●	
Yew, spreading English (TAXUS BACCATA)	5-10		●							●			●	●	●				●
DECIDUOUS																			
Artemesia, Silver Mound (ARTEMESIA SCHMIDTIANA)	3-10					●	●			●		●				●	●	●	
Catmint, mauve (NEPETA MUSSINII)	4-10					●	●	●		●		●			●	●			
Epimedium (EPIMEDIUM GRANDIFLORUM)	3-8			●		●		●		●		●	●		●				
Lily of the valley (CONVALLARIA MAJALIS)	3-7			●		●		●		●		●	●		●				
Rose, Max Graf (ROSA 'MAX GRAF')	5-10					●	●	●		●			●	●	●			●	●
Vetch, crown (CORONILLA VARIA)	3-10	●					●	●		●			●		●			●	
Woodruff (GALIUM ODORATA)	4-10			●		●		●		●	●	●			●			●	
SEMIEVERGREEN																			
Aaronsbeard St.-John's-wort (HYPERICUM CALYCINUM)	6-10	●					●			●	●		●		●		●	●	
Baby's tears (SOLEIROLIA SOLEIROLII)	9-10			●		●				●	●	●			●			●	
Bugleweed (AJUGA REPTANS)	3-10			●			●	●		●	●	●			●			●	
Chamomile (CHAMAEMELUM NOBILIS)	3-10						●			●	●	●			●			●	
Fescue, blue (FESTUCA OVINA GLAUCA)	3-9				●		●			●		●				●		●	
Mint, Corsican (MENTHA REQUIENII)	6-10		●	●		●	●			●	●	●			●			●	
Mondo grass (OPHIOPOGON JAPONICUS)	8-10			●			●			●	●	●			●			●	
Phlox, moss (PHLOX SUBULATA)	3-9		●			●	●	●		●	●	●			●	●	●	●	
Rose, memorial (ROSA WICHURAIANA)	5-10	●				●	●	●	●	●			●		●		●		●
Rose, sun (HELIANTHEMUM NUMMULARIUM)	5-10		●				●	●		●		●			●		●		

Choosing a ground cover. This chart lists 40 common ground covers by their English and Latin names, grouped according to foliage type—evergreen, deciduous or semievergreen. The first column in the chart lists the climatic zones (*map, page 122*) in which each plant thrives; semievergreen plants flourish widely but are green year-round only in Zones 8 to 10. Light and soil requirements are indicated by dots in the appropriate columns; these columns are left blank for plants that thrive in both moist and dry soil or in sun and shade. Many species have more than one special trait or can be propagated by more than one method; for these, multiple dots are entered.

Fast-growing Vines for a Dramatic Display

Because they are remarkably fast-growing and hardy, vines can cover large areas quickly. What is more, they create a uniquely dramatic green or variegated display because of the manner of their growth. Sending sinuous stems upward or outward, vines mature as long ribbons of foliage that can be trained and pruned to grow on solid walls, on open fences or on such special supports as trellises, arbors and archways *(pages 116-121)*.

Depending on how they are supported and where they are placed, vines can accent attractive landscaping features, screen unattractive ones, provide leafy shade over a sitting area, or offer a lush backdrop for decorative shrubs and flowers. With no support at all, some vines can serve as ground covers for areas too steep or too shady for a conventional lawn. In general, vines are ideal plantings for compact areas—they take up little ground space for their abundance of foliage—and for new gardens, where they fill an area long before slower-growing shrubs and trees can take over.

Many garden vines are descended from tropical plants and grow outdoors only in warmer regions of the United States; others, including such favorites as ivy and winter creeper, are hardy in cooler zones. The chart on the opposite page lists the growing zones for 43 of the most widely available vines, along with indications of each vine's most important characteristics: Is the foliage variegated or all green? Is the vine annual or perennial? Evergreen or deciduous? In some cases, the chart lists apparently contradictory characteristics. Some vines that are perennials in warm-weather zones become annuals in cooler climates and must be replanted every year. Similarly, some evergreen vines are deciduous in cooler zones.

The methods by which vines climb are an important consideration in choosing a specific vine to fill a landscaping need.

Botanists distinguish among more than 30 different climbing techniques that vines have developed to compensate for their inability to support themselves. Landscape designers and gardeners generally combine the 30 into the three major groupings listed in the chart.

Twiners, including akebia and wisteria, spiral upward, wrapping their stems around upright posts and vertical trellis supports. Clingers, such as Boston ivy and grapes, send out sticky rootlets or finger-like tendrils to hold fast to vertical or horizontal surfaces. And leaners, such as roses and most jasmines, do not really climb, but arch upward and droop unless they are draped over an upright support or secured with twine or with plant ties.

Almost all vines begin to grow soon after their deep root systems have had time to develop. The waiting period is brief for annuals—morning glories are a notably fast-starting species—but some of the perennials, such as wisteria, may need two or three years to get ready. If you want immediate shade from a new arbor, consider planting annuals adjacent to perennials for the first year or two.

Rates of growth vary considerably. In a single season of growth, the aptly named winter creeper extends itself only a few inches; the fox grape can reach out as far as 25 feet. For purposes of comparison, the chart defines slow growers as vines that grow less than a foot a year; medium growers from 1 to 5 feet, and fast growers more than 5 feet. Of course, differences in care, watering and climate can affect growth rates considerably; use the chart to get a relative idea of what to expect from a given vine.

One vine to avoid is the fastest grower of all, the incredible kudzu. Known as "the vine that ate the South," the kudzu's tentacles can grow a foot a day, overwhelming anything in their path, including trees, utility poles and an occasional

parked car. Not surprisingly, it is illegal to plant kudzu in many localities.

Most vines grow best in moist but well-drained soil that is mildly acid, between 6.5 and 7.0 pH. Annuals are usually planted as seeds and can often be started indoors during the winter, then transplanted outdoors in the spring. Perennials are usually sold as potted plants one or two years old and should be placed in a 2- to 3-foot-deep mixture of one part low-nitrogen (5-10-5) or no-nitrogen (0-10-10) fertilizer and two parts soil. These formulations initially stimulate root and stem development at the expense of foliage growth, but the trade-off is worthwhile for the future health of the plants.

Water newly planted vines well, and provide all vines with a thorough soaking every seven to 10 days during the growing season. During the hottest months, add a layer of mulch around the base of the vines to retain moisture.

Left alone, most vines tend to extend stems straight up without branching; they must be tied to horizontal supports and carefully pruned to promote horizontal growth. When plants are young, pinch off the stem tips just above the growth buds to encourage branching and dense growth. On mature plants, cut away excess growth at least once a year—preferably in late winter or early spring when the plant is dormant—and remove some of the stems near the center to stimulate growth in the outer stems.

Vines are remarkably healthy plants, requiring little protection from insects and disease. For most, an occasional spraying with a brisk jet of water is enough to discourage insects. Insecticides may be needed to repel severe attacks of aphids and Japanese beetles—particularly on grape vines—and to control euonymus scale, a pest that takes its name from the scientific name of its favorite vine, the winter creeper.

Characteristics of Vines

	Zones	Uses			Light		Traits						Growth rate			Climbing means			Foliage color	
		Ground cover	Shade	Screen	Full sun	Partial shade	Deciduous	Evergreen	Annual	Perennial	Fruits/berries	Flowers	Fast	Medium	Slow	Clinger	Leaner	Twiner	Green	Variegated
Akebia, five-leaf (AKEBIA QUINATA)	4-10	●	●	●	●	●		●	●		●	●						●	●	
Ampelopsis, porcelain (AMPELOPSIS BREVIPEDUNCULATA)	4-10	●	●	●	●		●			●	●		●			●			●	
Baby's tears (SOLEIROLIA SOLEIROLII)	9-10	●				●	●	●		●		●					●		●	
Black-eyed-Susan vine (THUNBERGIA ALATA)	8-10				●		●	●	●		●	●					●	●	●	
Bleeding heart (CLERODENDRUM THOMSONIAE)	10			●		●		●		●		●	●				●	●	●	
Bougainvillea, Brazilian (BOUGAINVILLEA SPECTABILIS)	9-10		●	●		●		●		●		●	●				●	●	●	
Cardinal climber (IPOMOEA MULTIFIDA)	3-10	●		●	●		●		●	●		●	●				●	●	●	
Clematis, 'Duchess of Edinburgh' (CLEMATIS FLORIDA)	5-10		●	●		●	●			●		●	●			●			●	
Clematis, Jackman (CLEMATIS JACKMANII)	5-10		●	●		●	●			●		●	●			●			●	
Clematis, 'Nelly Moser' (CLEMATIS PATENS)	5-10		●	●		●	●			●		●	●			●			●	
Clematis, sweet autumn (CLEMATIS PANICULATA)	5-10	●	●	●		●	●			●		●	●			●			●	
Crossvine (BIGNONIA CAPREOLATA)	6-10	●		●	●			●		●		●	●			●				●
Cup-and-saucer vine (COBAEA SCANDENS)	3-10		●	●	●	●	●		●			●	●			●			●	
Fig, creeping (FICUS PUMILA)	9-10		●	●		●		●		●			●			●			●	
Goldcup chalice vine (SOLANDRA GUTTATA)	9-10		●	●		●		●		●		●	●				●		●	
Grape, fox (VITIS LABRUSCA)	5-10		●	●		●	●			●	●		●			●				●
Guinea gold vine (HIBBERTIA SCANDENS)	9-10	●		●		●		●		●		●					●	●	●	
Honeysuckle, Cape (TECOMARIA CAPENSIS)	8-10	●	●	●		●		●		●		●	●				●		●	
Honeysuckle, goldflame (LONICERA HECKROTTII)	5-10	●		●	●	●				●		●					●	●	●	
Honeysuckle, Hall's (LONICERA JAPONICA 'HALLIANA')	4-10	●		●	●	●		●		●		●					●	●	●	
Honeysuckle, trumpet (LONICERA SEMPERVIRENS)	3-10	●		●	●	●	●			●	●	●					●	●	●	
Hydrangea, climbing (HYDRANGEA ANOMALA PETIOLARIS)	5-10		●	●		●	●			●		●			●	●			●	
Ivy, Algerian variegated (HEDERA CANARIENSIS 'VARIEGATA')	8-10	●		●		●		●		●			●		●	●				●
Ivy, Boston (PARTHENOCISSUS TRICUSPIDATA)	4-10	●		●		●	●			●	●		●			●			●	
Ivy, English (HEDERA HELIX)	4-10	●		●		●		●		●			●			●			●	
Ivy, grape (CISSUS RHOMBIFOLIA)	10		●	●		●		●		●			●			●			●	
Jasmine, Carolina (GELSEMIUM SEMPERVIRENS)	8-10	●	●	●		●		●		●		●	●				●		●	
Jasmine, common white (JASMINUM OFFICIANALE)	7-10		●		●	●	●			●		●	●				●		●	
Jasmine, star (TRACHELOSPERMUM JASMINOIDES)	9-10	●	●	●		●		●		●		●			●		●	●	●	
Lantana, trailing (LANTANA MONTEVIDENSIS)	9-10	●			●		●	●	●	●		●	●				●		●	
Morning glory, 'Heavenly Blue' (IPOMOEA TRICOLOR)	3-10		●	●	●		●		●			●	●				●	●	●	
Passionflower (PASSIFLORA ALATOCAERULEA)	7-10		●	●	●		●			●	●	●	●					●	●	
Periwinkle, common (VINCA MINOR)	4-10	●			●	●		●		●		●				●			●	
Periwinkle, greater (VINCA MAJOR)	8-10	●		●			●			●		●				●			●	
Plumbago, Cape (PLUMBAGO CAPENSIS)	9-10		●	●	●			●		●		●				●			●	
Rose, Banks' (ROSA BANKSIAE)	5-10		●	●		●		●		●		●				●			●	
Rose, 'Blaze' (ROSA 'BLAZE')	6-10		●	●		●	●			●		●				●			●	
Rose, memorial (ROSA WICHURAIANA)	5-10	●		●		●		●		●		●		●		●			●	
Silver fleece vine (POLYGONUM AUBERTII)	4-10		●	●		●	●			●		●	●					●	●	
Trumpet creeper (CAMPSIS RADICANS)	5-10		●	●		●	●			●		●	●			●			●	
Virginia creeper (PARTHENOCISSUS QUINQUEFOLIA)	3-10	●		●	●	●	●		●	●	●		●			●				●
Winter creeper, common (EUONYMUS FORTUNEI RADICANS)	5-10	●		●	●		●			●	●			●	●	●			●	
Wisteria, Japanese (WISTERIA FLORIBUNDA)	3-10		●	●	●		●			●	●	●	●					●	●	

Choosing a vine. This chart lists 43 selected vines by their common English names, followed by their more precise Latin names. The numbered zones, indicating where each plant can be grown outdoors, are keyed to the zone map on page 122. Read the dots horizontally to determine the characteristics of an individual vine; read the lines vertically to assemble a choice of plants that share a particular characteristic. Note that in two categories, Uses and Traits, the characteristics of a single species of vine may be indicated by more than one dot; in all other categories, one dot marks the predominant characteristic. For additional information on vines used as ground covers, see the chart on page 61.

3

Tall Trees and Massed Shrubs

A neat cut that can heal clean. The stubby, curved cutting blade of a pair of lopping shears slices easily through an unwanted branch; the same beveled blade will also trim the dead stub at lower left, leaving a clean wound that resists infection and heals easily. Such judicious pruning shapes trees and shrubs, fosters thick foliage and, above all, protects the health of the plants.

Small garden plants tend to be prized for either their beauty or their utility. Trees and their smaller cousins, the shrubs, combine both virtues—and more. They create a variety of delights: the rustle of wind in branches; the fragrance of blossoms and foliage; and a rich range of color, from the pale green buds of spring to the lush growth of summer and the finale of fiery autumn. But they have practical uses, too: Trees can screen a biting winter wind, shade a patio or a garden party, yield a harvest of nuts or syrup; shrubs serve as borders, windbreaks or high privacy fences.

Trees in particular have another, more elusive virtue. Their qualities and long lives inspire a deep human bond. People plant saplings for posterity, cherish mature trees for generations and mourn the passing of a gnarled, weatherbeaten hardwood almost as a death in the family. There are practical as well as sentimental reasons for this solicitude. Unlike smaller plants, which may require weekly care but seldom give major trouble, large woody specimens need something like the foresight and preventive care that physicians give their human patients. A sapling that develops a sharp V-shaped crotch rather than a U-shaped one should be pruned while young *(pages 66-69)*, for such a crotch will weaken the mature tree. Leaves may be seared by a nearby barbecue grill, impairing their ability to convert sunlight into energy. Root beds, which extend well beyond the circle marked by the outermost branches of a tree or hedge, must be protected from several hazards: Slight changes in grade level or drainage can inundate the roots or deprive them of water, a patio or walkway effectively suffocates any roots below it, and heavy construction machinery compacts the soil so densely that nutrients and water cannot reach the roots. Damage from such insidious hazards is slow to develop, but cumulative and eventually deadly.

Caring for trees and shrubs requires not only preventive care but vigilance and quick intervention. A broken or diseased branch should be cut off before infection can enter the ragged stump or invade healthy wood; if you suspect fungus or disease, clean the pruning tools afterward with denatured alcohol. Cuts and bruises of any sort—from nails, ropes, lawn mowers or whatever—expose the wood to pests and disease; trim away the ragged bark with a knife, leaving a vertical oval with a neat edge between the healthy bark and the wound. Potential attacks by pests and disease can be forestalled by fertilizing techniques that feed root systems directly *(pages 70-71)* and by chemical sprays *(page 72)*. All these measures entail only a modest investment of time, but they ensure a rich return in pleasure and usefulness—literally for generations, in some cases—from the dominant landmarks of a yard.

Techniques for Keeping a Tree in Good Health

Trees are rightly prized for their stature, their beauty of leaf, their fragrant blossoming in springtime and their cascades of red and gold in fall—but they offer more than esthetic value alone. Deciduous trees on the south side of a house shield it from the hot summer sun. Evergreens on the northwest form a barrier to the harsh winds of winter. And a row of low-growing trees along a busy road screens out traffic noise.

Like the houses they protect and adorn, trees need regular—and sometimes professional—care. Filling a hollow cavity or bracing limbs with guy wires requires expertise; thus, only a specialist should attempt such jobs. Similarly, cutting limbs from a perch high in a tree is dangerous for a novice; sawed limbs often kick back unpredictably and can knock an unwary worker to the ground.

Fortunately, the routine maintenance chores of pruning, fertilizing and pest control fall within the abilities of a homeowner. These three essentials of tree husbandry are especially crucial for young plants; a well-maintained sapling will grow into a strong, well-formed tree that will seldom need professional care.

Pruning improves the health of a tree, but like all surgery, it must be done judiciously. No matter how carefully a pruning cut is made, it wounds the tree; the key to good pruning lies in precise and minimal cuts that help the tree to use its natural healing mechanisms.

To defend itself, a tree walls off a wounded area with specialized cells and produces chemical barriers that prevent disease-causing organisms from invading healthy tissue. These cells and chemicals develop at the base of each branch in a swollen area called the branch collar. Pruning a branch flush to the trunk, a method recommended in the past, destroys protective cells in the collar, and the wound closes slowly, if at all. Cutting a branch too far from the trunk leaves a stub that conducts disease-bearing microorganisms into the tree; impeded by the stub, the tissue of protective cells will not be able to close the wound. Only pruning cuts made just outside the collar at the proper angle (opposite, bottom) will close properly.

Painting a pruning wound, a technique formerly believed to aid the closing process, offers no benefit to the tree, and heavy coatings retard closure. However, a thin coat of asphalt-based tree paint has a certain cosmetic value and it will not do any harm.

For the varied sizes and locations of tree limbs, you will need specialized pruning tools. Those illustrated on pages 68 and 69—a pruning knife, lopping shears, pruning saw and pole shears—will handle all the pruning chores you are likely to attempt.

Keep the blade of any pruning tool razor-sharp (page 12), so that it slices limbs cleanly without tearing or compressing the wood. To protect yourself from the cutting edge, wear heavy gloves when handling the tools. Wear eye protection when cutting overhead.

In general, the best seasons for pruning are late winter and early spring, before the buds open. Flowering trees, however, should be pruned just after the flowers fade, and broken or diseased branches should be removed immediately, whenever they are spotted.

To maintain vigorous normal growth, trees need a variety of chemical elements from the soil. The best way to supply a garden tree with essential elements is to fertilize it. Good tree fertilizers include manufactured mixtures and organic materials such as cottonseed meal, bone meal or blood meal.

Fertilizer can either be poured dry into holes near the roots or injected as liquid into the ground. Holes for dry fertilizer are generally drilled with an earth auger, which resembles a giant drill bit and is in fact driven by a conventional hand drill. Liquid fertilizer is spurted from a tool called a root-zone injector, driven by a garden hose. Apply dry fertilizer every year or two, in early spring. Liquid fertilizers, which disperse more quickly, can be applied several times a season, but never later than early summer; late fertilization encourages fall leaf growth, which is vulnerable to winter freezes.

In a third method, called foliar fertilization, liquid fertilizer is sprayed onto a tree's leaves, which absorb it directly and immediately. Foliar fertilization will perk up a tree within a week, but its dramatic effects are short-lived. It is best used in combination with root fertilization.

Pruned and fertilized trees are relatively resistant to most insects and diseases, but even a healthy tree can succumb. If a tree looks sickly or harbors bugs you do not recognize, send some affected leaves or bark to your extension service for diagnosis. The prescription is likely to be a spray-on chemical.

Chemical sprays are strong medicines that must be handled with care, but you can spray a tree up to 25 feet tall safely with the equipment shown on page 72. A larger tree calls for hiring a professional.

For trees up to 10 feet tall, use a pressurized canister—a 1½-gallon steel tank with a built-in pressure pump. A manual sprayer, which works much like a bicycle pump, has a reach of 25 feet or more. A third variation consists of a garden-hose attachment that automatically mixes insecticide and water; the sprayer itself is small, but it can deliver up to six gallons of solution between fillings.

Before using any insecticide or other spray, check into ordinances governing chemical spraying in your community. Study the instructions and cautions on the package label. Most insecticides must be mixed with water; dilute them exactly as directed. While spraying a tree, wear long sleeves, gloves, goggles and a hat. Keep children and pets out of the area, and do not permit them to walk near recently sprayed trees.

If you want to try a treatment that is nontoxic to pets and humans, a spray of dormant oil—a mixture of mineral oil and water—offers an alternative to strong chemical insecticides for controlling certain pests. Sprayed on a tree in early spring, before leaves emerge, the emulsion coats and smothers aphids, scales, mites and insect eggs. But read the label directions carefully: The oil can damage evergreens and certain species of beech, birch and maple.

Biological controls consisting of a pest's natural enemies offer another alternative to chemicals. A single ladybug will eat four dozen aphids a day; an invisible bacterium attacks gypsy-moth caterpillars but is harmless to other organisms. Ask your nursery operator or extension agent how to obtain such pest fighters in your area.

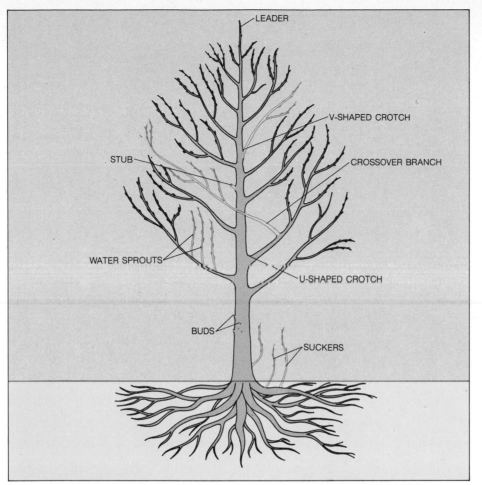

Labels on the tree diagram:
- LEADER
- V-SHAPED CROTCH
- STUB
- CROSSOVER BRANCH
- WATER SPROUTS
- U-SHAPED CROTCH
- BUDS
- SUCKERS

How to Prune a Tree

The basic guidelines. On a well-formed young tree, a straight central branch called the leader extends above all the other branches; the main limbs have U-shaped crotches, are evenly distributed around the trunk, and are spaced at least a foot apart. To maintain this strong, balanced framework, you must prune away the undesirable features, represented in white.

Remove any branches with a tight, V-shaped crotch; such a joint is inherently weak. Slender shoots called suckers or water sprouts, which grow from the limbs, trunk or roots of the tree and put out no lateral branches, are not part of the natural branch pattern; cut off these shoots and any buds on the trunk. Remove branch stubs and any dead or broken limbs, and thin out small branches that grow in toward the trunk or across larger limbs; these crossover branches will eventually rub against their neighbors, wearing away bark and causing wounds.

Mature trees have a few additional pruning requirements. Thin out inner branches periodically to admit light. On a deciduous tree, remove low limbs that prevent you from walking under the tree. The lower limbs on evergreen trees are usually left in place. On any tree, remove all dead, diseased or broken branches.

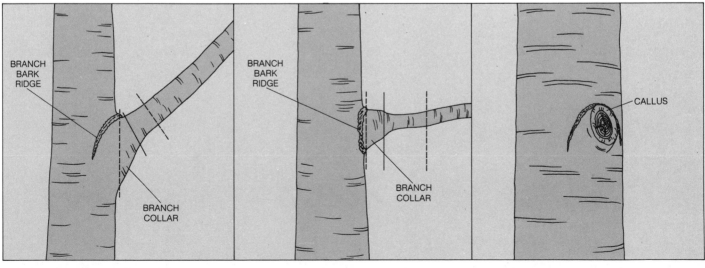

Labels on the lower diagrams:
- BRANCH BARK RIDGE
- BRANCH COLLAR
- BRANCH BARK RIDGE
- BRANCH COLLAR
- CALLUS

Proper pruning cuts. The structure of a tree dictates the correct spot and angle for cutting off a branch. A growing branch develops a thickened collar at its base, and a dark, raised saddle called the branch bark ridge forms on the parent branch or trunk. To remove a branch, cut outside of and at an opposing angle to the ridge, as indicated by the solid line *(above, left)*; do not cut into the collar itself or into the ridge, and do not make a cut so far out that it will leave a protruding stub *(dotted lines)*.

On evergreens and very young deciduous trees, the bark ridge may encircle the base of the branch, and the collar may be especially large and pronounced *(above, middle)*. In such a case, make a straight cut just outside the collar and parallel to the bark ridge *(solid line)*; be sure not to leave a stub beyond the collar, and take care not to cut into the ridge or the collar *(dotted lines)*. In a year or so, the edge of a pruning wound should form a hard callus *(above, right)*, and eventually this hard growth will close over the cut. If the callus does not form or forms incompletely, the pruning cut may have been improperly made or the tree may be too old or weak to respond well.

Two Tools for Small-scale Pruning

A knife to flick off sprouts. Use a pruning knife to slice off buds and small branches up to ¼ inch thick. Wearing heavy gardening gloves, set the knife's curved cutting edge on the top of a branch; press your thumb against the bottom of the branch, and turn the knife handle downward with a twist of your wrist *(arrow)*.

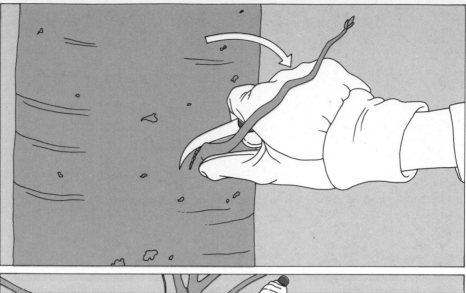

Cutting off small branches. To cut off a branch up to 1 inch thick, set the cutting blade of a pair of lopping shears on top of the limb, with the side of the blade against the trunk or supporting branch; then angle the lower blade away from the branch bark ridge and the branch collar, and bring the handles of the shears together in a single smooth motion. Do not twist the shears or use them to pull the branch away from the tree, and do not make repeated hacking cuts; if you find that you are resorting to any of these maneuvers, either the branch is too large for the tool or the blade is too dull for the job.

Sawing Off a Large Branch

1 Removing the branch. Before cutting a branch up to 3 inches thick, trim off secondary limbs to lighten the branch and to keep it from catching in the tree as it falls, then use a pruning saw to cut the branch itself in two separate stages. First, saw halfway through the underside of the branch, about a foot from the trunk; this cut will keep the bark from tearing when the branch falls. Next, an inch or two out from the first cut, saw down through the branch from the top; when the second cut is halfway through the branch, the limb will snap off, leaving a stub.

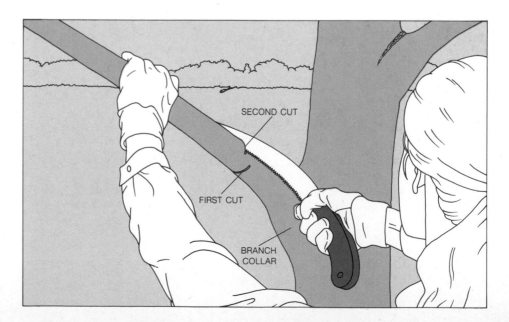

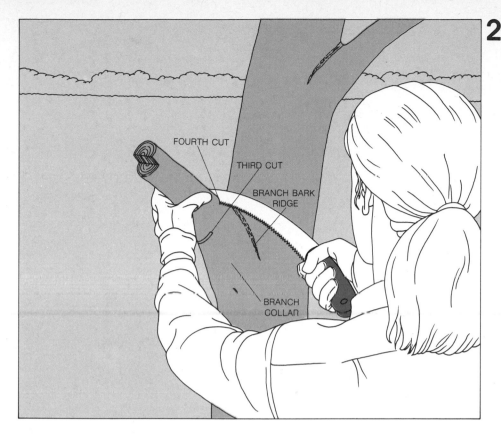

2 Trimming the stub. Saw a 1-inch cut in the underside of the stub, just outside the branch collar and at an angle opposite to that of the branch bark ridge. Then, supporting the stub with one hand, set the saw blade on the crotch of the stub *(left)*, just outside the branch bark ridge, and saw downward at an angle to meet the upward cut.

FOURTH CUT

THIRD CUT

BRANCH BARK RIDGE

BRANCH COLLAR

SAW BLADE

HOOK

CUTTING BLADE

PULLEYS

POLE

Pole Tools for High Pruning

Extendable shears. To reach branches up to 1 inch thick and up to 15 feet overhead, pole shears have a telescoping metal shaft or a set of wooden rods joined with metal hardware; the cord that works the cutting blade has a double pulley to increase leverage. Place the hook, located above the blade, over the base of the branch; wrap the cord once around the pole to keep the shaft from bowing, and pull on the cord to move the blade. It may be difficult or impossible to position the blade exactly for a properly angled cut, but be sure to cut close enough to the branch collar so that you do not leave a stub. If the cut branch hangs in the tree, pull it down with the head of the shears, but try not to break other branches.

Cut high branches up to 3 inches thick with the saw attachment *(inset)* of a pair of pole shears. Set the saw's teeth against the side of the branch, and move the blade in short up-and-down strokes; if the saw binds, start over from the other side. As with pole shears, it is hard to position the blade properly in relation to the branch collar and bark ridge, but you should be able to execute a smooth, straight cut without leaving a stub. If the branch is thicker than 1 inch, wear a hard hat.

Perforating the Ground to Fertilize Tree Roots

1 Mapping the holes. Lay a string or garden hose around the tree at the drip line—the line directly below the tree's outermost leaves. Mark a second circle about two thirds of the way in from the drip line to the trunk, and a third circle about the same distance outside the drip line. Allowing about 10 holes for each inch of the trunk's diameter, plan hole locations distributed evenly between the inner and outer circles *(inset)*.

Although it is not essential, you may use a garden trowel to lift out small divots of sod at each hole position. After drilling the holes and applying the fertilizer, you can cap the holes with the divots to preserve the looks of the lawn.

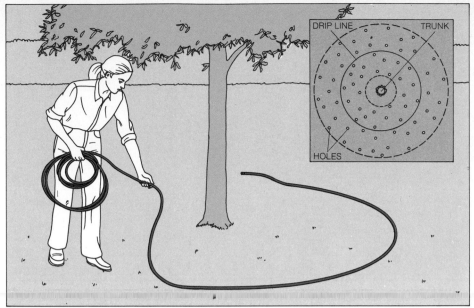

2 Using the earth auger. Clamp the auger into the chuck of an electric drill—a ¼-inch drill for an 18-inch auger, a ⅜-inch drill for a 24-inch auger. Steady the drill with both hands, push the tip of the auger into the soil and drill 2 to 3 inches straight down. Pull the drill out of the hole and let the dirt spin off, then repeat the process in the same hole, drilling 2 to 3 inches at a time until the length of the auger penetrates the soil.

3 Applying the fertilizer. For trees less than 6 inches thick, measure out 1 to 2 pounds of granular fertilizer per inch of trunk diameter; for larger trees, use 2 to 4 pounds per inch. (Follow the fertilizer label instructions if they differ from these recommended doses.) Mix the fertilizer with an equal amount of soil, sand or peat moss and, using a funnel to prevent fertilizer from spilling on the grass, pour about 1 cup of the mixture into each hole. Fill the hole to the top with soil, sand or peat moss; if you removed a divot before drilling, use it now to cap the hole.

Injecting Fertilizer by Water Pressure

1 Preparing a root-zone injector. Lay out the tree's drip line on the ground and indicate a location for an injection every 2 to 3 feet along the line. For a tree more than 4 inches in diameter with widespread branches, mark a second circle halfway in toward the trunk and plot injector locations along this circle (*inset*). Consult the directions on the fertilizer box to find the number of fertilizer cartridges needed for each inch of the tree's diameter. Calculate the total number of cartridges required, and divide this total by the number of injections to determine how many cartridges you will need for each injection. For example, if the tree needs a total of 45 cartridges and you plan to make 15 injections, allow three cartridges per injection.

To load the root-zone injector for one injection, unscrew the cap of the reservoir and drop in the required number of cartridges. If an injection requires more cartridges than the reservoir holds, you will have to replenish the supply as the fertilizer dissolves.

2 Using the injector. Close the water-flow control valve and connect the injector to the end of a garden hose. Adjust the spigot at the house to a medium flow, and open the control valve on the injector just enough to permit water to trickle out of the tube. Push the tube straight down into the soil; the flow of water will soften the dirt, allowing the tube to slip easily into the ground. For small trees with shallow roots, insert the tube about halfway into the ground; for large, mature trees, plunge it in to the hilt.

With the injector in the ground, adjust the control valve. For trees with shallow roots, set the valve at a point halfway between OFF and HALF ON; for more deeply rooted trees, set the control to HALF ON; for very large, well-established trees, start at HALF ON, then move the control to ON after the first minute of flow. Leave the injector in place until the measured amount of fertilizer has dissolved, then turn the water off at the control valve and pull the tube out of the ground.

DRIP LINE TRUNK

HOLES

WATER-FLOW CONTROL

GARDEN-HOSE CONNECTOR

Hand-pumped Tools for Small Batches of Spray

A pressurized canister for small jobs. To fill the canister, remove the pump assembly. Pour in some water and add liquid fertilizer or insecticide. Pour in the rest of the water needed to dilute the chemical. If you are using a powder, combine it with water in a bucket before pouring it into the canister to make sure it is completely mixed. Screw in the pump, and vigorously raise and lower the handle several times to pressurize the tank. As you spray, pump the handle each time the spray weakens. Aim the nozzle upward and squeeze the pistol grip to saturate the undersides of leaves. Adjust the fineness of the spray, if necessary, by twisting the nozzle tip.

A manual pump sprayer. Drop the screened intake end of the hose into the solution. Seal the nozzle with your gloved finger and pull the pump handle back to draw liquid into the hose. Remove your finger and push the handle forward. Repeat this priming operation until the solution sprays without spitting. Then aim the nozzle at the tree and pump the handle to spray the leaves. When you are finished, pump a quart of clear water through the sprayer.

NOZZLE

PISTOL GRIP

PRESSURE-PUMP HANDLE

NOZZLE

HANDLE

SPRAY SOLUTION

INTAKE SCREEN

Using a Garden-hose Sprayer

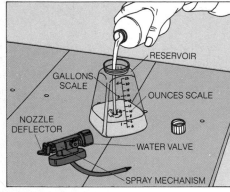

RESERVOIR

GALLONS SCALE

OUNCES SCALE

NOZZLE DEFLECTOR

WATER VALVE

SPRAY MECHANISM

1 **Filling the sprayer reservoir.** Pour in concentrated liquid fertilizer, measuring with the ounces scale on the reservoir's side. Add water until the mixture reaches the level on the gallons scale that indicates the amount of spray solution you will need. Screw on the spray mechanism, close the water valve and gently shake the sprayer.

2 **Using the sprayer.** Connect the sprayer to a garden hose and open the spigot. With the sprayer pointed at the tree, open the water valve on the sprayer. To control the length of the spray, adjust the garden-hose spigot. When spraying dormant oil, adjust the sprayer nozzle for a narrow stream, and saturate the trunk and limbs.

How to Move a Tree

A tree's size, weight and stability make it seem a permanent part of a landscape, but there are times when a tree must be moved. Small or young trees, for example, should be shifted out of the way of construction projects to protect their trunks and branches from injury and prevent their roots from being compacted by heavy equipment; the trees can be stored safely and replanted when the work is finished. A mature tree might be relocated permanently to fit a new landscape plan, and some trees must be moved from locations dangerous to their health—areas with poor drainage, unfavorable soil or extreme wind.

Trees up to 10 feet tall with trunks up to 3 inches thick can be moved with relative ease and can be expected to prosper after the move. Larger trees, however, are unwieldy and are more vulnerable to shock; the job of moving them should be evaluated—and, generally, performed—by a professional.

The best time to move a deciduous tree is in late autumn or early spring, when the tree is dormant; an evergreen can be moved at any time. If possible, cut the roots to their proper root-ball dimensions (top right) several months to a year in advance so that new feeder roots have time to form before the tree is moved. Do not cut the tap root—the main support root that runs straight down into the ground. At this point the tree will no longer be able to support its full complement of branches and foliage; to make up for the lost root capacity, prune away about a third of the branches.

When the time comes to move the tree, cut the tap root and wrap the root ball in burlap, either tied with twine or pinned with 2- or 3-inch nails. Tying with twine is somewhat simpler for beginners. Use a biodegradable material, such as cotton or hemp, which disintegrates after the tree is replanted; do not use plastic or nylon string, which would eventually strangle the roots. Professional nurseries generally pin the burlap with nails. The technique calls for more skill, but it is easier in the long run, particularly on large trees, because unlike tying, it does not require tilting the heavy root ball.

Uprooting a Tree—Safely

1 Pruning the roots. Using a spade with a well-sharpened blade, sever the roots in a circle 24 to 30 inches wide around the trunk. Push the blade into the ground at about a 30° angle toward the trunk, so that the root ball will taper. When you have cut the roots, prune the tree; take off about one third of the crown, but do not cut off the leader (page 67).

2 Digging out the tree. With a sharp spade, dig an 18-inch-deep trench just outside the cut made around the root ball, then thrust the blade of the spade horizontally beneath the tree and sever the tap root and other large roots. Next, working with a helper, lift the tree by the root ball and place the root ball in the center of a square of burlap.

Lifting an evergreen or any small tree with low branches may be easier if you work the burlap into the hole first, as for shrubs (page 92).

3 Bagging the root ball. To tie burlap around a root ball (*below, left*), draw the fabric up around the ball on all sides, tucking in the excess; then secure the burlap around the trunk with several turns of a length of twine. Run the twine under the ball in several directions, tilting the tree to get the string beneath it. When you have bound the root ball into a neat package, turn the twine around the trunk several more times and tie it off.

To pin burlap around a root ball (*below, right*), gather a corner of the fabric, folding the excess under, and pull it up tightly over the ball. Push a 2- or 3-inch nail through the fabric parallel to the top of the ball, then turn the nail back and thrust it through the fabric and into the ball. Continue gathering and pinning sections of burlap until you have bound the root ball snugly on all sides.

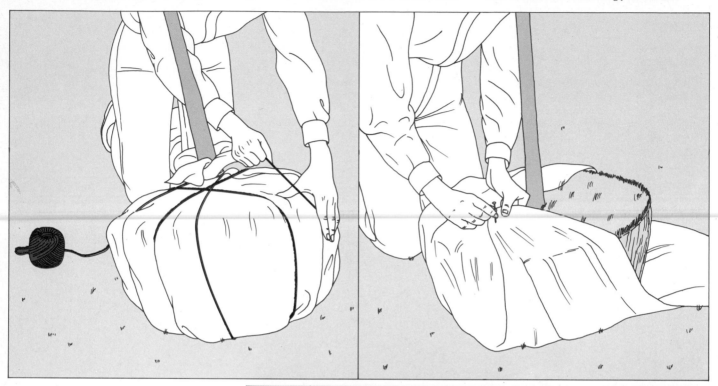

4 Storing the tree. At a spot that is shady and protected from wind, dig a hole half the depth of the root ball. Tip the burlap-wrapped ball into the hole, and pile a 6-inch layer of mulch over it. Water the mulch periodically to keep the root ball from drying out.

If you plan to replant the tree within a week or so, simply set the root ball in a shady spot and give it a good watering. Do not immerse it in water; the roots will rot if they get too wet.

MULCH

The Right Way to Plant a Tree

Trees are common symbols of immovability, yet almost every garden tree is moved at least once in its lifetime—from its birthplace, where it starts life as a seedling, to a new location in a homeowner's yard. For this crucial journey, the tree generally takes one of three portable forms: balled-and-burlapped, container-grown or bare-rooted.

A balled-and-burlapped tree, like a tree prepared for transplanting within a yard *(pages 73-74)*, is dug out of the ground, and its root ball is tightly wrapped in burlap. If you buy such a tree and do not intend to plant it at once, store it by the method shown at left below. Container-grown trees are seeded and grown in large metal cans or plastic buckets. Bare-rooted trees, usually sold by mail-order nurseries, are generally smaller, younger and less expensive than the other two types. But they are more vulnerable to injury because their roots, packed in moist peat moss or sawdust, or wrapped in plastic, are relatively unprotected.

Before buying a young tree in any form, use the climate map and species chart on pages 81-83 to find out which species thrive in your locality. Test the chemical composition of your soil *(pages 32-33)* and choose a tree that will flourish in it; as a rule, it is easier to buy a tree that matches your soil than to alter the soil to suit the tree.

At a nursery, look for signs of mishandling, such as scratched bark or broken branches, and of neglect, such as small, pale leaves or dry soil. A healthy young tree has dark, glossy, full-sized leaves and a full complement of branches growing from the top two thirds of its trunk. If you see more than one unhealthy looking tree, go to another nursery.

If a tree is container-grown, ask the nursery operator to loosen the container so you can see the roots. They should be thick and many-stranded at the bottom and should not protrude from the top of the soil surface or coil tightly around the root ball—signs of overcrowding. On a balled-and-burlapped tree, the root ball should feel firm and solid; crumbling soil indicates that the roots have been torn and may have dried out.

Before planting the tree, create an environment hospitable to it by conditioning the soil you dig out of the planting hole. An organic soil amendment, such as peat moss or compost, will help sandy soil retain moisture and enable clay-rich earth to drain more efficiently. A newly planted tree properly fertilized at the time of planting will not need additional fertilizer for at least a year.

Just after planting a bare-rooted or a balled-and-burlapped tree, prune about one third of the branches; a container-grown tree does not need pruning since it has not lost any of its roots. Wrap the trunk of all new trees with trunk wrap, a kind of layered bandage made of crepe paper and asphalt. The wrap expands as the tree grows, protecting the tender bark from the burning sun and from gnawing animals. Brace the tree *(page 80, Step 3)* to steady it and keep winds from loosening its roots in the new site. Finally, water the tree well; it should receive the equivalent of an inch of rainfall a week during the growing season. Allow the ground around the tree's base to dry out between each watering.

Planting a Balled and Burlapped Tree

1 **Digging the hole.** Using a pointed spade, dig a round hole twice as wide and one and a half times as deep as the root ball. Toss the soil onto a sheet of burlap, plastic or canvas, which will serve as a firm surface for mixing in soil conditioners and slow-release fertilizer *(overleaf)*.

2 Conditioning the soil. Add peat moss, compost or another organic amendment to the soil removed from the planting hole, mixing the ingredients thoroughly with the spade. Try to confine the mixing job to the sheet—the ingredients will be difficult to handle on grass or ground covers. For loamy soil, add one part peat moss or compost to two parts soil; for clay-rich soil, add one part peat moss and one part sand to one part soil. For sandy soil, add one part peat moss to one part soil. Any of the three soil types should also receive an admixture of slow-release fertilizer, in the amount recommended by the fertilizer manufacturer.

3 Making a base for the tree. Fill the planting hole about a third full with the conditioned soil mixture, then tamp the mixture firmly down with your feet. Add more mixture and tamp again, repeating the procedure until you have built a firm base one third the depth of the hole.

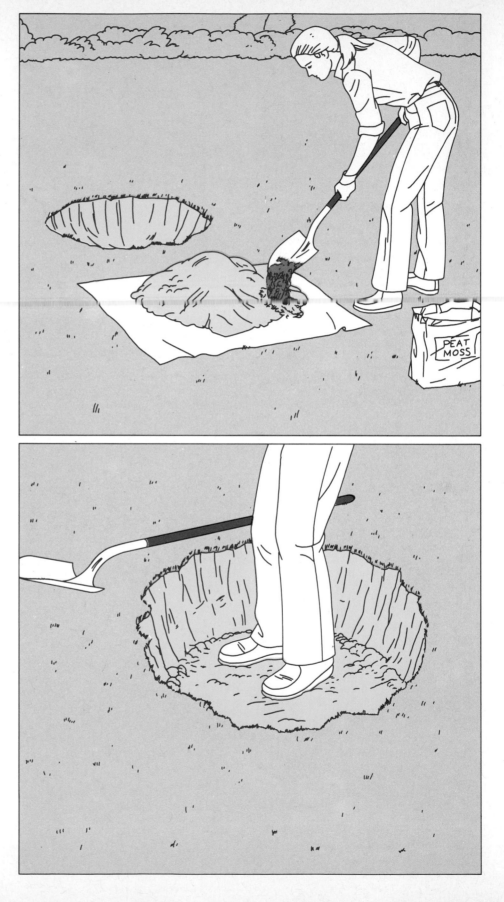

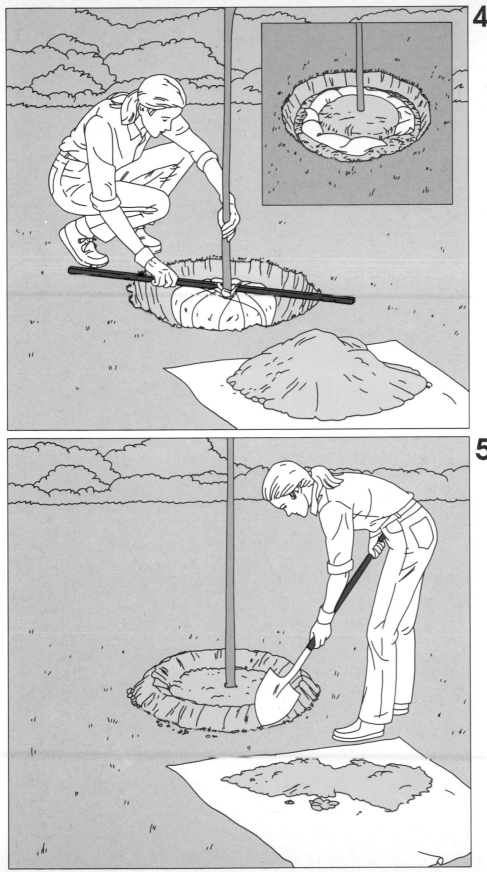

4 **Positioning the tree.** Set the root ball in the center of the hole, hold the tree trunk vertical and lay a board or yardstick across the hole to check the level of the ball. The ground at the top of the hole should be even with the top of the root ball or slightly higher, but not above the tree's original soil level as indicated by a darker band of bark at the base of the trunk. If the tree is too high or too low, lift it out and remove or add soil at the bottom of the hole, then reposition the tree. In poor drainage areas, it is best to plant the tree a little high.

Add soil mixture to the hole, tamping it down with your foot, until its level is two thirds the depth of the hole, then loosen the burlap at the top of the root ball (inset) and fill the hole with water. When the water has drained away, fill the hole to ground level with soil mixture and tamp the mixture firmly.

5 **Forming a basin of soil.** To prevent water from draining away from the roots of the tree, build a dike of soil 2 to 4 inches high around the edge of the planting hole. Fill this basin with water; then, when the water has seeped into the ground, pile a 3-inch-deep mulch of ground bark or wood chips inside the basin and around the trunk.

Planting a Container-grown Tree

1 Taking the tree from the container. Prepare a planting hole by the method shown on pages 75-76. Then, for a metal container, don heavy leather gloves and cut the container from top to bottom in three or four places with a pair of tin snips. Spread the strips of metal and lift out the root mass without knocking off the soil. A plastic container will usually slide off easily if you rap it gently or squeeze and release its sides; if it does not, cut it with tin snips or heavy scissors.

2 Arranging the roots. Untwine the coiled roots around the root mass so that they will not strangle each other or grow in circles. Loosen the exposed roots slightly and gently tease apart the root mass with a trowel or spade. Using pruning shears, trim off broken roots at the first joint above the break. Set the root mass in the planting hole, spreading out the roots. Build a soil basin around the tree, water the tree well and fill the basin with mulch (*page 77, Step 5*).

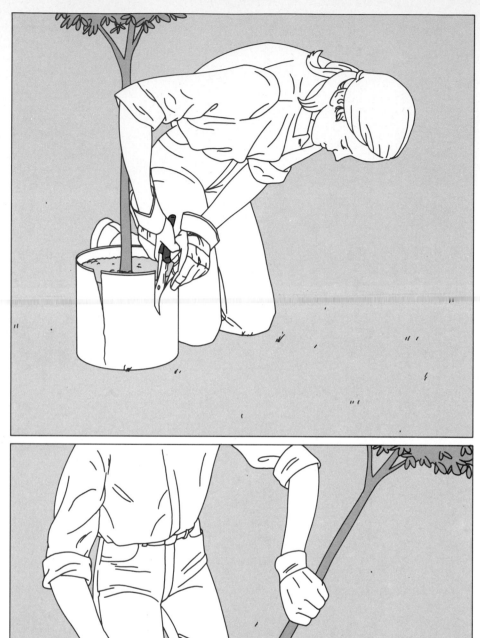

Planting a Bare-rooted Tree

1 **Positioning the roots.** Dig and prepare a planting hole *(pages 75-76)*, about one and a half times as deep as the length of the tree's longest root; make the hole about as wide as it is deep. Build up a cone-shaped mound of soil at the center of the hole. Set the tree in the hole and spread the roots out over the mound. Lay a yardstick or a board across the hole *(page 77, Step 4)* to set the soil-level mark on the tree trunk even with or a little higher than ground level. If the mark is below ground level, remove the tree and make the soil mound higher.

2 **Filling the hole around the roots.** Hold the tree in place and scoop the soil mixture into the hole and around the roots. Press the soil down with your hands, using your fingers to work the soil around the roots to eliminate air pockets. Add soil to two thirds the depth of the hole, then fill the hole with water. After the water has drained away, fill the hole up to ground level. Build a soil basin and fill it with water, then add mulch *(page 77, Step 5)*.

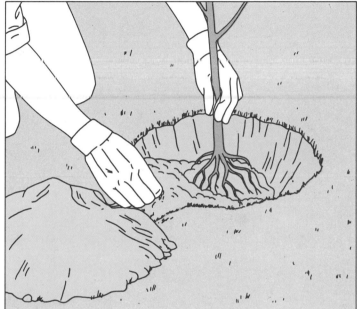

Caring for the Newly Planted Tree

1 **Pruning the branches.** Immediately after planting a balled-and-burlapped or bare-rooted tree, trim away one third of its branch structure with pruning shears. Remove all weak or poorly positioned branches *(page 67)*, but do not cut the main or top leader branch. Also, do not prune a container-grown tree or any tree that was pruned for you at the nursery.

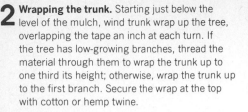

2 **Wrapping the trunk.** Starting just below the level of the mulch, wind trunk wrap up the tree, overlapping the tape an inch at each turn. If the tree has low-growing branches, thread the material through them to wrap the trunk up to one third its height; otherwise, wrap the trunk up to the first branch. Secure the wrap at the top with cotton or hemp twine.

Keep the trunk wrap in place for two years. Inspect the twine every few months and loosen it whenever it begins to cut deeply into the tape; the tape will expand as the tree grows, but the twine must be loosened periodically to prevent it from cutting into the tree's bark.

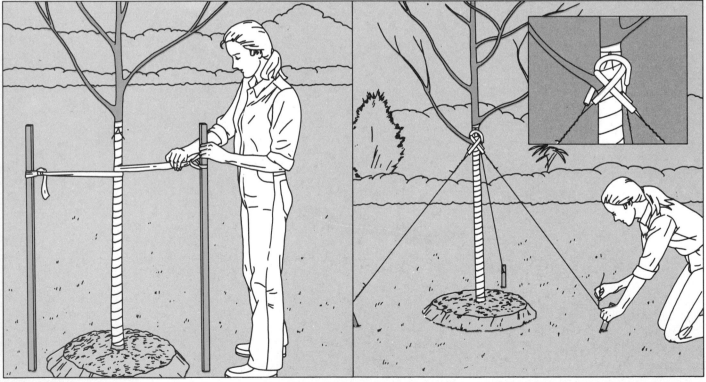

3 **Bracing the tree.** For a tree with a trunk less than 3 inches thick (above, left), position a pair of 6-foot, 2-by-2 posts outside the soft soil of the planting hole, and drive the posts 2 feet into the ground. Tie the end of a strip of cloth near the top of a post, loop it once around the trunk and tie the other end to the opposite post. To brace a tree with a trunk 3 inches or more in diameter (above, right), drive three notched stakes into the ground just outside the planting hole and at equal distances from the trunk and from each other. Thread the end of a guy wire through a 1-foot-long segment of rubber hose, wrap the hose around the trunk above the crotch of a branch and twist the end of the wire back around itself; loop the other end of the wire around the notch in a stake. Add two more wires and hose segments (inset). All the wires should be straight but not taut; leave enough extra length at the stakes so that the wires can be loosened as the tree grows.

Where Trees Prosper

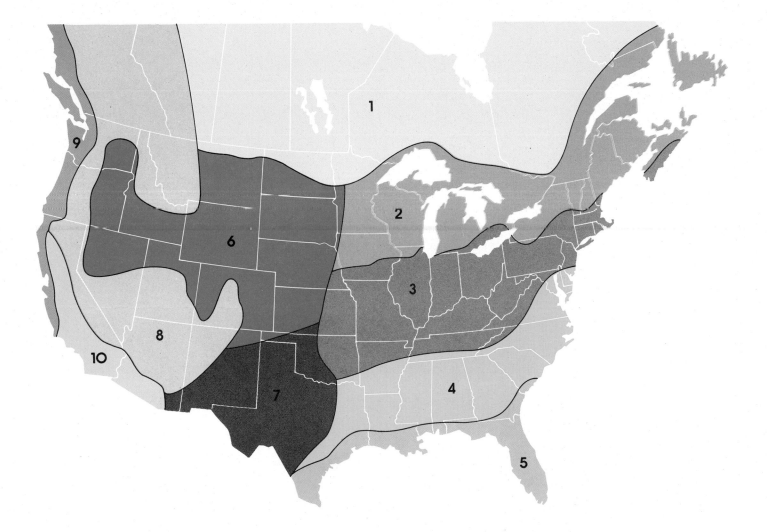

Matching trees to environment. This map divides the United States and southern Canada into 10 numbered zones, each characterized by a unique pattern of temperature, rainfall, altitude and soil. Use the map in conjunction with the chart of tree species on pages 82-83. In the chart, the name of a tree is followed by one or more numbers indicating the zone or zones in which the tree normally flourishes. Locust, for example, thrives in zones 1 through 10, while California black oak does well only in zones 9 and 10. Though they are reliable as a general guide, the map and accompanying chart are not foolproof, because local conditions can vary within one zone. For example, areas at high altitudes tend to be colder than lowlands, and large bodies of water moderate swings of temperature. Always consult your local agricultural extension service or a local nursery to be sure that a particular tree will do well in your yard.

A Selection of Yard and Garden Trees

DECIDUOUS TREES

	Zones	Moist	Dry	Acid	Alkaline	Light shade	Full sun	To 25 ft.	Over 25 ft.	Slow	Moderate	Fast	Columnar	Rounded	Weeping	Spreading	Conical	Flowers	Fruit or seeds	Leaf color	Bark
Ash, European mountain (SORBUS AUCUPARIA)	2-4,6-10					●	●				●			●				●	●	●	
Ash, Modesto (FRAXINUS VELUTINA GLABRA)	3-5,7,9,10		●		●	●	●				●			●						●	
Ash, Moraine (FRAXINUS HOLOTRICHA 'MORAINE')	3-5,7-10					●	●				●	●	●	●							
Bauhinia, Buddhist (BAUHINIA VARIEGATA)	5,10	●		●		●	●				●			●		●		●		●	
Birch, European white (BETULA PENDULA)	1-4,6-10	●				●	●				●				●	●				●	●
Catalpa, common (CATALPA BIGNONIOIDES)	3-10						●				●			●				●	●		
Cherry, double-flowered mazzard (PRUNUS AVIUM PLENA)	2-10					●	●				●					●		●			
Cherry, Higan (PRUNUS SUBHIRTELLA)	3,4,9,10					●	●				●							●			
Cherry, paperbark (PRUNUS SERRULA)	3,4,9,10					●	●				●			●							●
Cherry, Yoshino (PRUNUS YEDOENSIS)	2-4,9,10					●	●				●					●		●			
Chestnut, Chinese (CASTANEA MOLLISSIMA)	3,4,7,9,10			●		●	●				●			●				●	●		
Chinaberry (MELIA AZEDARACH)	3-5,7,10				●	●	●				●			●							
Crab apple, Arnold (MALUS ARNOLDIANA)	2-4,6-9	●	●			●	●			●				●				●	●		
Crab apple, Dolgo (MALUS 'DOLGO')	1-4,6-9	●	●			●	●				●							●	●		
Crab apple, Flame (MALUS 'FLAME')	1-4,6-9	●	●			●	●				●			●				●	●		
Crab apple, Red Jade (MALUS 'RED JADE')	2-4,6-9	●	●			●	●				●				●			●	●		
Crab apple, Zumi (MALUS ZUMI CALOCARPA)	3,4,7,9	●	●			●	●				●					●		●	●		
Dogwood, flowering (CORNUS FLORIDA)	3-5,7,9,10	●	●	●		●	●				●			●		●		●	●	●	●
Dogwood, Kousa (CORNUS KOUSA)	3-5,7,9,10	●	●	●		●	●				●					●		●	●	●	
Franklinia (FRANKLINIA ALATAMAHA)	3-5,9,10	●		●		●	●			●							●	●		●	
Fringe tree (CHIONANTHUS VIRGINICUS)	2-7,9,10	●				●	●			●				●				●			
Golden-rain tree (KOELREUTERIA PANICULATA)	3-10				●	●	●					●		●				●			
Golden shower (CASSIA FISTULA)	5,10						●					●		●				●			
Hawthorn, Toba (CRATAEGUS MORDENENSIS 'TOBA')	1-4,6-10					●	●			●				●				●			
Hawthorn, Washington (CRATAEGUS PHAENOPYRUM)	2-4,6-10					●		●		●				●				●	●		
Hop hornbeam, American (OSTRYA VIRGINIANA)	2-7,9	●						●	●	●				●							
Hornbeam, European (CARPINUS BETULUS)	3,4,7,9					●		●	●	●			●							●	●
Jacaranda, sharp-leaved (JACARANDA ACUTIFOLIA)	5,10			●			●				●					●		●		●	
Jerusalem thorn (PARKINSONIA ACULEATA)	4,5,10					●	●				●					●		●			
Jujube (ZIZYPHUS JUJUBA)	4,5,7,10				●		●			●						●			●		
Katsura tree (CERCIDIPHYLLUM JAPONICUM)	2-10	●				●		●			●									●	
Laburnum, Waterer (LABURNUM WATERERII)	3,4,6-10	●			●		●			●				●				●			
Lilac, Japanese tree (SYRINGA AMURENSIS JAPONICA)	1-4,6-9	●				●	●			●				●				●			
Locust, Idaho (ROBINIA 'IDAHO')	1-10		●		●		●				●		●	●				●			
Magnolia, saucer (MAGNOLIA SOULANGIANA)	3-5,7,8,10	●		●			●			●						●		●			
Maple, Amur (ACER GINNALA)	1-3,6,8,9						●				●			●				●	●	●	
Maple, Japanese (ACER PALMATUM)	3,4,9,10	●			●	●	●		●	●				●						●	●
Maple, paperbark (ACER GRISEUM)	3,4,9					●	●		●	●				●						●	●
Maple, vine (ACER CIRCINATUM)	3,4,9,10	●			●	●			●	●						●		●	●	●	●
Mesquite, honey (PROSOPIS GLANDULOSA)	4,5,7,10		●		●	●	●				●					●		●	●		
Oak, California black (QUERCUS KELLOGGII)	9,10			●		●	●				●					●			●	●	
Olive, Russian (ELAEAGNUS ANGUSTIFOLIA)	1-10					●	●				●			●				●	●	●	
Parasol tree, Chinese (FIRMIANA SIMPLEX)	5,10	●				●	●				●						●	●		●	

Choosing a suitable tree. This chart lists 83 small and medium-sized ornamental trees suitable for a garden, patio or yard; 54 are deciduous trees, 14 are narrow-leafed evergreens and 15 are broad-leafed evergreens. The first column gives the common English names of the trees in alphabetical order, followed by their technical Latin names; the second lists the geographical zone or zones in which each tree grows best (map, page 81). Special requirements for moisture, soil and light are indicated by dots; in each category, trees without distinct preferences are not marked by dots. In the column for Growth Rate, a slow-growing tree is one that adds less than 12 inches to its height annually; a

	Zones	Soil		Soil pH		Light		Height		Growth rate			Shape					Special traits			
		Moist	Dry	Acid	Alkaline	Light shade	Full sun	To 25 ft.	Over 25 ft.	Slow	Moderate	Fast	Columnar	Rounded	Weeping	Spreading	Conical	Flowers	Fruit or seeds	Leaf color	Bark
Pear, Bradford (PYRUS CALLERYANA 'BRADFORD')	2-10						●	●		●						●	●	●	●	●	
Pistache, Chinese (PISTACIA CHINENSIS)	5,10			●		●		●			●			●					●	●	
Plum, Pissard (PRUNUS CERASIFERA ATROPURPUREA)	2-10					●	●				●			●				●	●	●	
Poinciana, royal (DELONIX REGIA)	5					●		●			●					●		●	●		
Redbud, eastern (CERCIS CANADENSIS)	2-10	●				●		●			●	●		●				●	●		
Serviceberry, apple (AMELANCHIER GRANDIFLORA)	2-4,6-9	●					●				●			●				●	●	●	
Silver bell, Carolina (HALESIA CAROLINA)	3-5,9,10	●		●		●			●		●			●	●			●			
Snowbell, Japanese (STYRAX JAPONICA)	3-5,9,10	●				●		●			●			●				●			
Sorrel tree (OXYDENDRUM ARBOREUM)	3-5,9,10	●		●		●	●				●					●		●		●	
Tallow tree, Chinese (SAPIUM SEBIFERUM)	5,10					●		●			●					●			●	●	
Walnut, Hinds black (JUGLANS HINDSII)	9,10					●		●			●			●					●		

NARROW-LEAVED EVERGREENS

	Zones	Soil		Soil pH		Light		Height		Growth rate			Shape					Special traits			
		Moist	Dry	Acid	Alkaline	Light shade	Full sun	To 25 ft.	Over 25 ft.	Slow	Moderate	Fast	Columnar	Rounded	Weeping	Spreading	Conical	Flowers	Fruit or seeds	Leaf color	Bark
Arborvitae, Douglas (THUJA OCCIDENTALIS DOUGLASII PYRAMIDALIS)	1-4,6,8,9	●				●	●				●						●				
Cedar, California incense (LIBOCEDRUS DECURRENS)	3-5,9,10	●					●				●					●				●	●
Cedar, Japanese (CRYPTOMERIA JAPONICA)	3-5,9,10	●		●		●					●					●				●	●
Cypress, Italian (CUPRESSUS SEMPERVIRENS STRICTA)	4,5,7,10		●				●		●		●						●			●	●
Cypress, moss sawara, false (CHAMAECYPARIS PISIFERA SQUARROSA)	2-4,9,10	●					●		●		●						●				
Fir, China (CUNNINGHAMIA LANCEOLATA)	4,5,9,10			●			●				●					●			●	●	●
Juniper, blue column (JUNIPERUS CHINENSIS COLUMNARIS)	2-10		●			●	●		●								●				
Pine, Japanese black (PINUS THUNBERGII)	2-4,7,9,10		●			●		●			●				●		●		●		
Pine, Norfolk Island (ARAUCARIA HETEROPHYLLA)	5,10	●		●			●		●		●						●				
Pine, Tanyosho (PINUS DENSIFLORA UMBRACULIFERA)	2,3,8,9		●			●	●	●			●					●			●		
Pine, umbrella (SCIADOPITYS VERTICILLATA)	3,4,9,10		●			●	●		●		●						●			●	
Podocarpus yew (PODOCARPUS MACROPHYLLUS)	4,5,9,10	●			●	●					●		●							●	
Spruce, Serbian (PICEA OMORIKA)	2,3,6,8,9						●		●	●							●		●		
Yew, Irish (TAXUS BACCATA STRICTA)	3,4,9,10			●			●		●	●			●				●		●	●	

BROAD-LEAVED EVERGREENS

	Zones	Soil		Soil pH		Light		Height		Growth rate			Shape					Special traits			
		Moist	Dry	Acid	Alkaline	Light shade	Full sun	To 25 ft.	Over 25 ft.	Slow	Moderate	Fast	Columnar	Rounded	Weeping	Spreading	Conical	Flowers	Fruit or seeds	Leaf color	Bark
Ash, shamel (FRAXINUS UHDEI 'MAJESTIC BEAUTY')	10	●			●	●		●			●					●					
Camphor tree (CINNAMOMUM CAMPHORA)	5,10						●		●		●					●			●	●	●
Cootamundra wattle (ACACIA BAILEYANA)	10		●			●	●				●			●				●		●	
Elm, Chinese (ULMUS PARVIFOLIA)	3-5,7,9,10					●		●			●			●	●						
Holly, English (ILEX AQUIFOLIUM)	3-5,9,10			●		●		●	●					●					●	●	
Horsetail beefwood (CASUARINA EQUISETIFOLIA)	5,10						●		●		●					●		●			
Laurel (LAURUS NOBILIS)	4,5,9,10					●		●		●						●		●	●		
Loquat (ERIOBOTRYA JAPONICA)	4,5,7,9,10	●				●					●					●		●	●	●	
Oleander (NERIUM OLEANDER)	5,7,10	●				●	●	●			●			●				●			
Olive, common (OLEA EUROPAEA)	5,10		●			●	●	●			●			●				●	●	●	●
Orange, sweet (CITRUS SINENSIS)	5,10	●				●	●	●			●			●				●	●		
Osmanthus, holly (OSMANTHUS HETEROPHYLLUS)	3-5,7,9,10		●			●		●			●			●				●		●	
Pepper tree, California (SCHINUS MOLLE)	10					●		●			●				●			●	●		
Photinia, Fraser (PHOTINIA FRASERI)	4,5,7,9,10					●		●			●			●				●	●	●	●
Pineapple guava (FEIJOA SELLOWIANA)	5,10	●					●				●			●				●	●	●	

moderate growth rate is between 1 and 2 feet a year; fast growth is 3 feet or more a year. Tree shapes sometimes vary within a single species; in the Shape column, each variation is indicated by a dot. Variation is wider and more common in the special characteristics, such as striking leaf color or unusual bark, which give a tree a distinctive appearance; here, too, multiple dots may appear on the chart, indicating variations within a species.

Shrubs: Beautiful, Versatile, Easy to Maintain

Of all the elements in a landscape, shrubs are surely the most versatile. They serve as backgrounds for gardens, low dividers to separate the yard into different areas, and thick, tall screens for privacy. They are equally diverse in their decorative effects, ranging from bursts of floral brilliance to perennially green displays; and with just a little training or trimming, they can add a variety of shapes and textures to the yard.

Happily, these all-purpose plants are among the easiest to care for. A simple program of feeding, watering, weeding, pruning, and in some climates protecting the shrub from winter weather, will make shrubs luxuriant during the growing season and keep them healthy all year long.

Throughout the spring and summer, give them a long, slow watering every two weeks—every 7 to 10 days during dry spells. Add fertilizer to the beds just before or during spring growth, but not in midsummer or late summer; the nutrients stimulate new growth that will not have time to harden before winter.

Add mulch or compost to the beds of all shrubs, not only to provide nutrients, but also to keep the soil cool in summer and warm in winter and to inhibit weed growth. You can buy shredded pine bark or other organic mulch by the bag at garden centers; alternatively, you can use pine needles, leaves or grass clippings from the yard or create a true compost heap of your own (page 35). Whatever material you choose, simply spread it in a 2- to 3-inch layer around each plant and renew it in the spring and fall.

If mulch or compost alone fails to control weeds, you must either pull them by hand or eliminate them with chemical weed killers before they rob plants of nutrients. A local garden center or nursery can tell you which chemicals work best against the weeds in your area.

Pruning is the most time-consuming task in shrub care, but few tasks are more important. For one thing, pruning eliminates damaged and diseased wood that can imperil a plant's health, sometimes in unexpected ways. Crossing branches, for instance, can abrade each other, leaving the plant vulnerable to infection; such branches, along with all damaged, dead or diseased wood, should be cut off. Pruning also encourages new growth and—especially in roses—boosts flower, fruit and foliage production by reducing the number of limbs that must be sustained by the roots and circulatory system. Finally, pruning keeps the shrub in bounds and shapes it.

Four simple hand tools will enable you to meet these objectives easily and efficiently. You will need a pair of hand pruners, to clip small branches that are within easy reach; loppers, to remove larger branches several feet above your head; hedge clippers, to snip off leaves and twigs when you shape a bush; and a small pruning saw, to cut stems too thick for the lighter-duty tools.

Prune your shrubs in stages, several times a year. In the spring, remove any parts of the shrub that have been damaged by winter weather, and do some light shaping and trimming. For shrubs such as azaleas, lilacs and viburnums, which flower in the spring on old wood, wait until the blossoms have wilted before you undertake the spring pruning. Shrubs such as abelias, hydrangeas or honeysuckles, which flower in summer or autumn on new wood, can be pruned at any time during the winter, during the months up to midspring, or in summer after they have flowered.

Throughout the summer, shape and trim shrubs lightly every week or two; then, about the time of the first frost, give the plants a heavy cutting. After the shrubs have flowered, snip off about one third of the older stems at ground level, so that each plant is completely regenerated every three years or so.

As winter approaches, some shrubs may need protection from wind, cold and snow. To determine which of your plants to protect, check the chart on pages 94-95 and the climate-zone map on page 122. A local nursery can supply advice about specific shrubs; a neighbor may also be a good source of information about plants that need help to get through the winter.

Some methods of protecting shrubs are shown on page 89. For the best results, use these methods during the period between the first killing frost of autumn and the first hard freeze of winter. In a sudden spell of severe cold, you may also want to protect plants temporarily: Wrap them in burlap or even throw a blanket over them, but remove such makeshift shields as soon as the cold snap abates.

Heavy, wet snow is especially damaging to evergreen shrubs. After a storm, knock the snow off with a broom or a stick, or shake the shrub gently to dislodge the snow. Take care, however, not to snap the branches, which may be brittle with the cold.

Winter damage to broad-leaved evergreens frequently results from leaf transpiration, the technical term for water loss by evaporation. To minimize such damage, thoroughly soak the ground around the plants in the autumn, before the first hard freeze; then place heavy mulch, such as a mixture of leaves and straw, around the stem over the tops of the roots, keeping the mulch in place with a cylinder of wire. A commercial antitranspirant—a waxlike substance that can be sprayed onto the shrub periodically during the winter—will also help to hold moisture in the leaves.

Using Shrubs in a Landscape

A variety of roles. Used alone or in combination, shrubs create an extraordinary range of effects. Planted close together, a number of shrubs of the same species form a hedge to provide a screen against a neighbor or the street. A hedge can be a background for gardens or sculpture, or define an area for play or outdoor living. A border, like a hedge but with a variety of species, can be used in the same ways; but it

is less effective as a background because of its diverse and distracting colors and textures.

In the language of landscape architecture, a group is an island of plants rising above the ground. In the example shown here, consisting of several shrubs around a tree, the shrubs offset the vertical effect of the tree; other examples might be combinations of variously sized and col-

ored shrubs chosen for intrinsic beauty. A specimen—a single plant with a noteworthy quality, such as a profusion of flowers, imposing size or a particularly pleasing shape—is usually placed where it can be seen from inside the house as well as from the yard. An accent plant can, for example, be the focal point of a border or group, or it can add grace notes at a corner of the house or beside the front door.

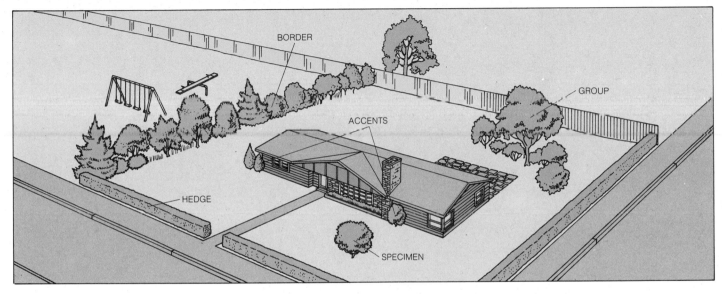

BORDER

GROUP

ACCENTS

HEDGE

SPECIMEN

SCUFFLE HOE

Routine Care to Keep Shrubs Healthy

Stirring up the soil. Before weeding a shrub bed, cultivate the soil with a scuffle hoe to loosen weeds and break up compacted soil. Push the point of the hoe (*inset*) into the ground, keeping the blade parallel to the soil, then work the blade forward and backward at a depth of about 1 or 2 inches; do not work so deeply that you catch roots. After weeding the bed, use the hoe again to smooth out the soil.

Getting water to the roots. Give large plants a long, slow soaking, keeping the water aimed at the roots. For one common soaking method, attach the hose end to a sprinkler extension, a wandlike device that breaks up the stream of water to shower the bed gently (*below, left*). Alter-natively—particularly for hedges, groups or young plantings—you can use a soaker hose (*below, right*), a length of hose pierced by tiny holes, from which water seeps or sprinkles according to the pressure. Soaker hose is available in lengths of 25 feet and longer.

SOAKER HOSE

Spreading mulch. To keep shrub roots from drying in the summer sun and to prevent deep frost penetration in the winter, spread an even layer of mulch on the bed. If you use dense mate-rial, such as wood chips or ground bark, pile the mulch about 2 inches deep; if you use a looser material, such as pine needles or oak leaves, make the mulch layer about 3 inches thick. Cover the entire shrub basin, but do not pack the material tightly against the plant stems; moisture in the mulch could produce rot.

Pruning: The Kindest Cuts of All

Trimming for shape. Grasp a branch just be-low a bud and set the cutting blade of a pair of pruning shears ⅛ to ¼ inch above the bud. Holding the shears at a 45° angle slanting away from the bud, sever the branch with a smooth, firm squeeze of the handles. To ensure that new branches grow away from the main trunk, as indicated by the dashed lines in this example, make each cut at a lateral bud—that is, a bud pointing outward from the side of a shoot.

Trimming hedges. To speed the trimming of a formal hedge, use electric or battery-operated clippers. Stretch a level string tightly between posts at the ends of the hedge to indicate the level of the cut. Then hold the clippers flat at the level of the string and draw them across the hedge top; do not poke the tip of the clippers into the hedge. As an alternative, use hedge shears, as shown in the inset.

If any long shoots are growing into a gap in the hedge, cut the shoots back with pruning shears to stimulate thick growth that will fill the hole.

Shape an informal, relatively irregular hedge as you would a shrub, using pruning shears and trying to create a natural, feathery appearance; take special care to prune out any branches that have grown faster than the others.

Trim both formal and informal hedges narrower at the top than at the bottom, to permit sunlight to reach the base of the hedge. After trimming a hedge, shake it to dislodge the clippings, then rake the clippings away.

Removing damaged wood. Use pruning shears to cut away dead, broken or diseased branches. Be sure to cut all the way back to healthy wood—either at a point just above a lateral bud or, as in the example at left, flush with the nearest healthy stem.

Thinning for health and light. Remove all weak, misshapen or crossing stems, using pruning shears, lopping shears (*right*) or a small curved saw, according to the thickness of the wood. Then cut up to one third of the healthy stems from the center of the shrub to allow light to reach the interior foliage. In both stages of the job, remove entire branches at a main stem or cut through a main stem at the ground.

The Right Way to Prune Roses

Cutting for more and better blossoms. Rose bushes need regular and extensive pruning to produce strong shoots and large flowers. In the fall, cut back every branch by a third of its length; cut away dead wood, small shoots and crossing branches; and thin the interior branches. After this pruning, the bush should be about two thirds of its original size, as indicated by the area shown in solid color at left, above.

In the spring, cut away every bit of wood that has been killed or damaged by winter weather. Also pare off weak, stringy branches and cut back all main branches to sound stems at least ⅜ inch thick. The spring pruning should leave a bowl-shaped plant with several main stems, as shown in solid color at right, above.

During the growing season, prune roses as you would any other shrub, cutting out dead and damaged wood and small branches.

88

Helping Shrubs to Get Through the Winter

Protecting a shrub from wind and snow. To protect a low-growing shrub, such as heather, cover the plant with branches and trimmings from needle-bearing evergreens *(below, left)*. A discarded Christmas tree is a good source for these clippings.

For medium-height shrubs that are exposed to the full force of the wind, build a shelter of stakes and burlap to the full height of the shrub *(center)*. First, drive several stakes in a tight circle all around the plant, then staple the burlap to the stakes; the burlap should hug the branches,

compressing them slightly. Tie needled evergreens with cord or twine to prevent heavy, wet snow from settling on the branches and breaking them: Starting at the bottom, wrap the line around the shrub tightly enough to hold the branches upright *(right)*.

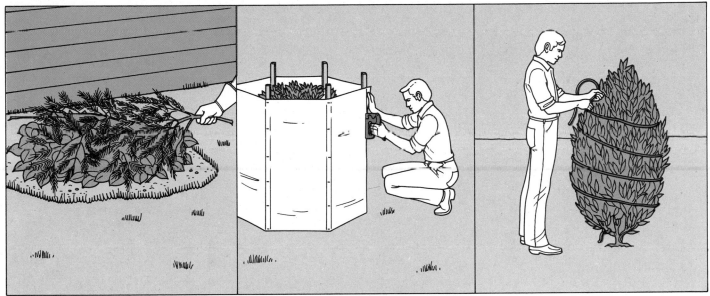

A shield for shrubs beneath an eave. A sloping shelter on a frame of 2 by 3 boards prevents the snow that slides off a roof from damaging shrubs along a house wall. Drive one pair of 2-by-3s, about a foot taller than the shrubs, into the ground behind the shrubs at the house wall. Put up a second, shorter pair in front of the shrubs. Connect the tops of each pair crosswise with 2-by-3s, and roof the structure with scrap boards spaced 4 to 6 inches apart.

Putting Plants in New Places

Because they grow quickly and can be set in place for immediate effect, transplanted or newly planted shrubs are ideal for making rapid changes in a landscape. For the most part, they are planted in much the same way as trees *(pages 75-79),* although you can save time in planting a hedge by digging a trench and setting in all the plants at once. The general rule, applicable to nearly every hedge species, is to space new shrubs at 3-foot intervals; slow-growing shrubs, such as hollies, or those with a strongly upright form, such as yews, can be planted closer together. When buying shrubs for a hedge, get a few extras and grow them elsewhere in the yard so that you will have them on hand if a shrub in the hedge dies.

New shrubs for plantings are available from a variety of sources. The most convenient, though also the most expensive, is a nursery. Choose a reputable one, which sells healthy shrubs acclimated to your region, and examine the shrubs carefully. They will come in one of three ways: with the roots in a ball of dirt wrapped in burlap, with the roots bare, or rooted in a large plastic container. Check a balled and burlapped plant to see that the ball is intact, weed-free and moist. Bare roots should be creamy white, not dark and foul-smelling. On any new shrub the leaves should be shiny and full, and the main stem should be centered above the root system; a lopsided stem will produce a lopsided top and a weak root system.

Transplanting shrubs is harder work than getting them from a nursery, but the transplanted shrub is free, and moving a shrub away from a location can sometimes be as desirable as adding one elsewhere. Transplanting is best done in early spring or early fall; first, water the shrub generously two days before the move—to soften the dirt around the roots—and tie up the branches with twine.

Propagating new plants from existing ones is a third source of shrubs. Although propagating, like transplanting, is free—or better than free, since you get two or more plants for the price of one—a year or more may pass before you get the plant you want. Choose the parent plant with care; the new shrub will be an exact duplicate of the one from which it is propagated, with all of the good and bad characteristics of its forebear. Azaleas, roses, aucubas and many other shrubs can be propagated by the cutting method shown on page 58; for others, such as forsythia or rhododendrons, use the method called ground layering *(page 93).* When in doubt about the appropriate method for a shrub, consult a nursery or your local agricultural extension service.

Whether you are planting, transplanting or propagating, have the hole ready for the shrub in advance. If you cannot plant the shrub immediately, store it in a cool, shaded place and keep the roots moist. Do not store a bare-rooted shrub in this way for more than a week; if you must wait longer, lay the shrub in a trench, cover its roots with dirt, and keep it watered until it is planted.

Discarding an Unwanted Shrub

1 Digging out the roots. Cut off most of the shrub's branches with pruning shears, but leave the main stem or a small clump of main stems 2 to 3 feet long to serve as a handle. Use a mattock to cut a circle about 2 feet in diameter around the shrub and down through the root system, then undercut the shrub with a spade or digging bar and pull the plant out by the stems. Proceed immediately to Step 2.

2 Refilling the hole. Hold the root ball of the shrub over the hole and, with a spading fork or other sharp tool, scrape all of the dirt from the roots back into the hole. Fill the hole with additional soil and tamp the soil, then add still more soil to form a loose mound about 4 to 6 inches high; the mound will settle naturally in two to three months, leaving the area level.

Transplanting a Shrub

1 Defining the digging area. Using the point of a spade, scratch a circle around the plant and directly under the outer edge of the foliage; then, with the blade facing toward the plant, plunge the spade 8 to 9 inches deep into the soil along the outline of the circle. In the same way, scratch and cut a second circle, wider than the first by the width of the spade blade.

2 Cutting out the root ball. Dig out the dirt between the two circles to the level of the shrub's major roots, generally about 18 inches down. Working around the root ball from different directions, undercut the shrub with the spade; then carefully scratch and chop the soil beneath the shrub until the ball comes loose. A small shrub can be taken from the hole now; for a larger shrub, go on to Step 3.

3 **Wrapping the root ball.** When the roots are free, push against one side of the root ball to tip the shrub, and stuff several folds of burlap into the gap (*below, left*). Let the ball roll back, and tip it in the opposite direction; then grasp the burlap and pull it under the ball (*below, right*). Lift the edges of the burlap and tie them tightly around the stem of the shrub with some twine.

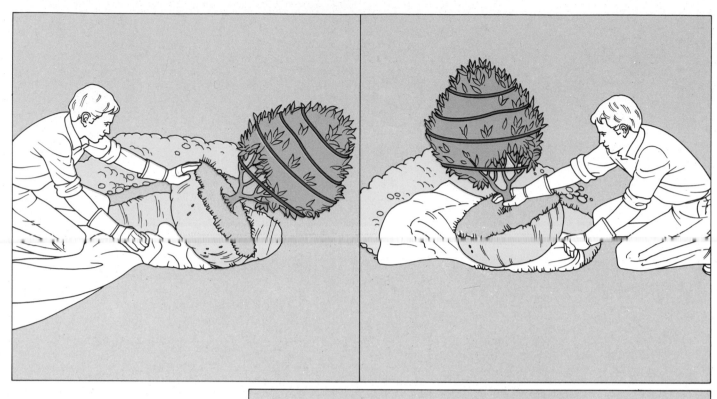

4 **Pulling out the shrub.** Grasp the burlap at the top of the root ball and lift the shrub out of the hole; you may need a helper for medium- or large-sized shrubs. Set the shrub on a sheet of plastic or hardboard, and slide the sheet along the ground to the desired location. Following the steps shown on pages 75-77, plant the shrub; to allow for settling, set the roots 1 to 2 inches shallower than their original depth.

Prune the transplanted shrub to compensate for roots lost during digging; also remove any broken branches and shape the plant.

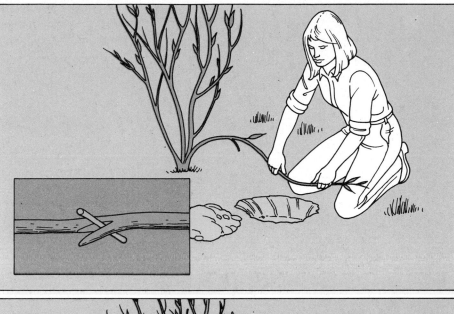

Propagating Shrubs by Layering

1 **Wounding the branch.** In early spring, bend a healthy lower branch of the plant to be propagated until it touches the ground about one foot from its tip. Dig a dish-shaped hole 6 inches deep at that spot.

Bend the branch into the hole. At the point in the branch that touches the center of the hole, cut diagonally halfway through the branch from below, using a pruning knife or a sharp pocket knife, and wedge the wound open with a pebble or a matchstick *(inset).* Sprinkle the open wound with rooting powder, a synthetic hormone that is available at nurseries and garden centers.

2 **Anchoring the branch.** Pour a mixture of equal parts of topsoil, peat moss and sand into the hole to a depth of 2 inches. Bend the branch back into the hole with the wound facing downward and anchor the branch in position with two crossed sticks; beyond the sticks, bend the branch up so that it rises about 6 inches above ground level. Cover the branch and fill the hole with the soil mix. Water the soil mix thoroughly and place a rock atop the crossed sticks to hold them in place.

3 **Separating the new shrub.** After about a year, dig out the buried branch and gently push away some soil to check for new roots. If the wound has produced 3 to 5 good roots, sever the branch to free the new root ball from the main plant. If the wound has not yet produced enough new roots, rebury the branch until fall and check again.

Once a satisfactory set of roots has been produced, push gently on the root ball to slant the roots away from the tip of the branch, then plant the propagated shrub as you would any other shrub. Tilt the ball as you set it into the hole, pointing the branch tip upward.

A Selection of Garden Shrubs

FLOWERING

	Zones	Hedge	Ground cover	Moist	Dry	Acid	Sun	Shade	Under 3 ft.	To 6 ft.	Over 6 ft.	White	Yellow-orange	Pink-red	Blue-purple	Spring	Summer	Fall	Fruit	Foliage	Fragrance
Acacia, rose (ROBINIA HISPIDA)	5-9		●			●	●			●				●		●	●				
Almond, flowering (PRUNUS TRILOBA)	5-9					●				●				●		●			●	●	
Azalea, catawba (RHODODENDRON CATAWBIENSE)	3-10			●		●		●		●				●	●	●					
Azalea, Exbury hybrid (RHODODENDRON)	5-8			●		●				●		●	●	●		●				●	
Azalea, flame (RHODODENDRON CALENDULACEUM)	4-10			●		●				●			●	●		●					
Azalea, pinxter-bloom (RHODODENDRON NUDIFLORUM)	3-8			●		●				●				●		●					
Barberry, Japanese (BERBERIS THUNBERGII)	4-10	●					●			●		●							●		
Barberry, Mentor (BERBERIS MENTORENSIS)	5-10	●					●			●		●									
Beauty bush (KOLKWITZIA AMABILIS)	4-9						●			●				●		●			●		
Broom, hybrid (CYTISUS HYBRIDS)	6-10					●	●	●	●	●		●	●	●		●					●
Buckeye, bottle-brush (AESCULUS PARVIFLORA)	4-10						●				●	●					●	●			
Butterfly bush, fountain (BUDDLEIA ALTERNIFOLIA)	5-10				●						●				●		●				●
Cherry, Cornelian (CORNUS MAS)	4-8						●				●		●			●			●		
Cherry, western sand (PRUNUS BESSEYI)	3-6				●		●			●		●				●					
Chokeberry, black (ARONIA MELANOCARPA)	4-10							●		●		●				●			●		
Chokeberry, brilliant (ARONIA ARBUTIFOLIA BRILLIANTISSIMA)	4-10						●			●		●				●			●		
Cinquefoil, bush (POTENTILLA FRUTICOSA)	2-9				●		●		●				●	●			●	●			
Cotoneaster, early (COTONEASTER ADPRESSA)	4-10				●		●			●		●				●			●	●	
Cotoneaster, horizontal (COTONEASTER HORIZONTALIS)	5-10		●		●		●		●			●		●				●	●		
Cotoneaster, Sungari (COTONEASTER RACEMIFLORA)	3-10				●		●			●		●				●			●	●	
Crape myrtle (LAGERSTROEMIA INDICA)	7-10	●		●			●			●		●		●			●		●		
Daphne, February (DAPHNE MEZEREUM)	4-9							●		●				●	●	●			●		●
Deutzia, slender (DEUTZIA GRACILIS)	4-9	●						●	●			●				●					
Enkianthus, redvein (ENKIANTHUS CAMPANULATUS)	4-9			●	●					●				●		●				●	
Forsythia, border (FORSYTHIA INTERMEDIA)	5-9	●								●			●			●					
Hazelnut, curly (CORYLUS AVELLANA CONTORTA)	4-9									●			●			●				●	
Honeysuckle, Amur (LONICERA MAACKII)	2-9									●		●				●			●	●	
Honeysuckle, Tartarian (LONICERA TARTARICA)	3-9									●				●		●			●		
Honeysuckle, winter (LONICERA FRAGRANTISSIMA)	5-9						●	●		●		●				●			●		●
Hydrangea, peegee (HYDRANGEA PANICULATA)	4-9		●							●		●					●	●			
Jasmine, winter (JASMINUM NUDIFLORUM)	6-9					●				●			●			●					
Kerria (KERRIA JAPONICA)	4-9							●		●			●			●	●	●	●		
Lilac, common (SYRINGA VULGARIS)	3-7						●			●	●	●		●	●	●					●
Mock orange, Lemoine (PHILADELPHUS LEMOINEI)	5-9						●			●		●					●				●
Pearlbush, common (EXOCHORDA RACEMOSA)	5-9					●				●	●	●				●					
Photinia, Oriental (PHOTINIA VILLOSA)	4-8						●			●		●				●			●	●	
Plum, beach (PRUNUS MARITIMA)	3-7				●		●			●		●				●			●		
Privet, Amur (LIGUSTRUM AMURENSE)	3-9	●					●			●		●					●		●		
Privet, Regel (LIGUSTRUM OBTUSIFOLIUM)	3-9	●					●			●		●					●		●		
Privet, vicary golden (LIGUSTRUM VICARYI)	4-9	●					●			●		●					●		●	●	
Pussy willow (SALIX DISCOLOR)	2-9		●			●			●	●				●		●					
Quince, hybrid flowering (CHAENOMELES HYBRIDS)	6-10	●			●		●		●	●				●	●	●			●		
Rose, Japanese (ROSA RUGOSA)	2-10				●		●			●				●		●	●	●	●	●	●
Olive, Russian (ELAEAGNUS ANGUSTIFOLIA)	2-9	●			●		●				●		●				●		●	●	
Snowberry (SYMPHORICARPOS ALBUS)	3-9	●						●		●				●			●		●		
Spirea, bridal-wreath (SPIRAEA PRUNIFOLIA)	4-10	●							●	●		●				●				●	
Spirea, Bumalda (SPIRAEA BUMALDA)	5-10						●		●					●			●			●	

Flowering shrubs

	Zones	Hedge	Ground cover	Moist	Dry	Acid	Sun	Shade	Under 3 ft.	To 6 ft.	Over 6 ft.	White	Yellow-orange	Pink-red	Blue-purple	Spring	Summer	Fall	Fruit	Foliage	Fragrance
		Uses		Soil			Light		Height			Flower color				Flower season			Special traits		
Spirea, Ural false (SORBARIA SORBIFOLIA)	2-8			●						●	●	●					●				
Spirea, Vanhoutte (SPIRAEA VANHOUTTEI)	4-10	●								●	●	●				●					
Summer sweet (CLETHRA ALNIFOLIA)	3-10			●		●				●	●	●					●			●	●
Sweet shrub (CALYCANTHUS FLORIDUS)	4-10			●						●				●	●	●				●	●
Tamarisk, five-stamened (TAMARIX PENTANDRA)	2-10					●				●				●			●				
Viburnum, fragrant snowball (VIBURNUM CARLCEPHALUM)	5-9	●								●	●	●				●			●	●	●
Viburnum, Marie's doublefile (VIBURNUM PLICATUM)	5-9	●								●	●	●				●					
Viburnum, Siebold (VIBURNUM SIEBOLDII)	4-9									●	●	●				●					
Weigela, hybrid (WEIGELA)	5-9									●	●			●		●					
Winter hazel, fragrant (CORYLOPSIS GLABRESCENS)	5-9			●		●				●		●	●		●	●				●	●
Witch hazel, Chinese (HAMAMELIS MOLLIS)	5-9			●						●		●	●		●	●				●	●

Choosing a flowering shrub. This chart, which begins on the opposite page, lists 58 flowering shrubs by their common English names, followed by their botanical Latin names. The numbered zones in which each shrub can be grown are keyed to the zone map on page 122. To find the characteristics of each shrub, follow the lines across the page to the dots under the headings. Some plants are listed without dots in some categories. Under Uses, dots are entered only for plants highly specialized as hedges or ground covers. In the Soil and the Light columns, a dot indicates a strong preference or a requirement; the absence of dots indicates that a plant adapts to a variety of soil and light conditions.

Evergreen

	Zones	Lawn specimen	Hedge	Screen	Ground cover	Fruits or berries	Moist	Dry	Acid	Alkaline	Under 1 ft.	To 3 ft.	To 6 ft.	To 10 ft.	White	Yellow-orange	Pink-red	Green	Dark green	Yellow-green	Blue-green
		Uses					Soil				Height				Flower color				Foliage color		
Arborvitae, Berckman's golden (PLATYCLADUS ORIENTALIS)	4,5,7,9,10		●	●				●					●				●		●		
Bearberry (ARCTOSTAPHYLOS UVA-URSI)	1-3,6,8-10				●	●	●	●	●		●						●		●		
Box, edging (BUXUS SEMPERVIRENS SUFFRUTICOSA)	3-5,9	●	●					●				●									●
Camellia, common (CAMELLIA JAPONICA)	4,5,9,10	●	●					●	●				●		●		●		●		
Cypress, false slender hinoki (CHAMAECYPARIS OBTUSA)	2-4,9,10	●						●						●			●				
Cypress, false thread sawara (CHAMAECYPARIS PISIFERA)	2-4,9,10	●						●					●				●			●	
Fire thorn, Laland (PYRACANTHA COCCINEA)	2-10			●		●							●	●	●				●		
Holly, American (ILEX OPACA)	3-5,9,10			●		●			●					●					●		
Holly, Burford (ILEX CORNUTA)	4,5,9,10			●		●							●						●		
Holly, Japanese (ILEX CRENATA)	3-5,9,10			●		●							●						●		
Juniper, Gold Coast (JUNIPERUS CHINENSIS AUREA)	2-10	●			●							●								●	
Juniper, tamarix (JUNIPERUS SABINA)	2-10				●							●									●
Juniper, Wilton carpet (JUNIPERUS HORIZONTALIS)	1-4,6-10				●						●										●
Laurel, mountain (KALMIA LATIFOLIA)	2-5,9	●					●		●				●				●		●		
Nandina (NANDINA DOMESTICA)	3-5,7,9,10				●	●						●	●		●				●		
Grape, Oregon holly (MAHONIA AQUIFOLIUM)	2-7,9,10					●						●				●		●	●		
Pine, Mugo (PINUS MUGO)	1,3,6,8,9	●	●		●							●							●		
Spruce, dwarf Alberta (PICEA GLAUCA)	1-3,6,8,9	●	●	●									●						●		
Tea tree (LEPTOSPERUM SCOPARIUM)	9,10		●					●					●				●		●		
Yew, spreading English (TAXUS BACCATA REPANDENS)	2-4,9,10	●	●					●				●							●		

Choosing an evergreen shrub. This chart lists 20 evergreen shrubs by their common names, then by their botanical names. The numbered zones in which each evergreen shrub can be grown refer to the zone map on page 81. The lack of a color indication under Flower Color means that the species does not bloom conspicuously. In all other respects the dotting system follows that of the chart on flowering shrubs, above.

Brightening a Landscape with Beds of Flowers

Unlike lawns, trees and shrubs, which enhance a landscape in a more or less permanent way, flowers are grace notes—short-lived splashes of color that come and go faster than the seasons. Whatever the character of a yard, however, there is room for the color and variety of flowers. They can be tucked along a house foundation, massed in an isolated bed or displayed in a thick, bright border along the edge of an area.

When choosing flowers for your own yard, consider their color, height, flower size, length of life and time of blooming. Tall flowers belong in the back rows of a bed or border, medium-height plants in the middle, shorter ones in front. In an isolated bed, tall flowers may be planted in the center, with heights tapering down to the edges. Such a well-ordered bed not only shows all the flowers to their best advantage, but helps ensure that every plant gets the daily sunshine it needs in order to thrive.

In length of life, flowers fall into three groups: annuals, biennials and perennials. Annuals complete their entire life cycle in a year. The seeds or seedlings are put into the ground in the spring; the flower germinates, grows and blooms; then the plant dies in the fall. Biennials have a two-year life span. They spend their first year germinating and growing, their second growing and flowering.

Perennials live for three or more years. Their hardy roots live underground all

Colors for All Seasons

A bed for a sequence of blossoms. The flower bed shown at right in spring, summer and fall produces color in all three seasons and includes evergreen foliage for the winter months. It consists chiefly of perennials, including some spring bulbs for extra color. A similar sequence of displays can be achieved with many different combinations of flowers, including annuals and biennials, if the plants are chosen for a wide range of flowering seasons.

In this example, the clematis and cotoneaster along the back wall bloom in the spring (top). The peonies in the middle row and the candytuft in the foreground are also in bloom, along with bulbs: tulips, daffodils and hyacinths.

In summer (middle), the climbing rose, tall phlox, and loosestrife provide color at the back of the bed. The middle row is especially rich in plants that blossom, including the gay-feather, day lily, black-eyed Susan, common yarrow, speedwell and bee balm. At the front of the garden, the coral-bells create a low border of attractive foliage and color, and the tiny blossoms of the lavender cotton sharply define the front edge of the bed. At this point in the year, the plantain lily has large gray-blue leaves and the miscanthus, a type of ornamental grass, is about 5 feet tall; neither will bloom until fall.

In the fall (bottom), the roses still bloom, but the Japanese anemones have become the major feature of the bed. Day lilies continue to bloom into September and the miscanthus produces large white plumes. The plantain lilies provide color through the middle of the bed and the candytuft blooms again at the front. The carnations may continue to bloom and the fall chrysanthemums are in flower. The cotoneaster will have bright red berries in the fall and winter, and a fall-blooming species of clematis will add color.

winter and send up new growth in spring. Although some bulbs must be dug up in the fall and stored over the winter, they, too, are technically perennials.

Flowers can be bought at a nursery or garden center or ordered from the bumper crop of catalogues mailed out every winter. Look for healthy green leaves, stocky stems and a good root system. It is tempting to purchase plants in full bloom, but those with few flowers are usually fresher and better. Bulbs should be firm and free of blemishes or mold.

Set out perennials and annuals in the spring, in beds that have been prepared in advance. To grow perennials from seed, start them indoors in pots or flats well before spring. Annuals, which grow faster, can be grown in flats *(page 56)* or sown outdoors, directly in the ground. Hardy bulbs should be planted in the fall to bloom the following spring; tender bulbs should be planted in spring to bloom later in the year. To plant bulbs, set them pointed end up at the depth specified on the package or, if no directions are given, at a depth equal to 3½ times the thickness of the bulb.

In fall, annuals must be dug up and disposed of; a compost heap *(page 35)* is the ideal place. Perennials reappear without replanting, but they do need some end-of-season care. Every two or three years—when the blooms begin to get less vigorous—dig up the plants and divide them as you would ground covers *(page 59)*. If the central part of a perennial has died, discard that portion and replant the healthy stems from the edges of the clump. After two or three frosts and at a time when the top of the soil is frozen, cover perennials with mulch to insulate the ground; the blanket of mulch interrupts the freeze-thaw cycle that causes the earth to heave and break roots.

Preparing Perennials for the Winter

Cutting and covering the plants. After two or three frosts, cut the foliage of herbaceous, or fleshy, perennials about 2 inches above the ground with hedge shears or pruning shears. Cover the stubs with a light layer of evergreen cuttings, pine needles or straw. Woody perennials should be pruned to remove dead foliage and flowers, but they do not require mulch.

Two Ways of Planting Bulbs

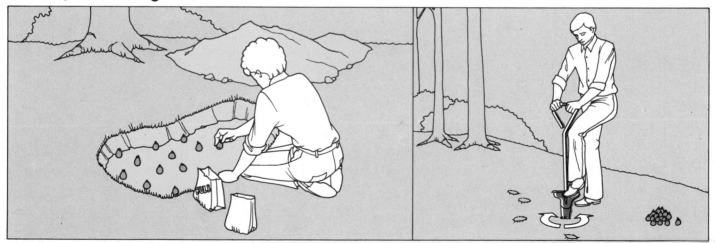

Bulbs by the bed or singly. To make an entire bed of bulbs, dig out the soil to a depth 1 inch greater than the planting depth recommended for the bulbs. Work a mixture of fertilizer and humus into the soil in the bottom of the bed *(above, left)*, then spread some of the excavated soil 1 inch deep over the mixture and press the bulbs into the soil, wide end down and about 5 inches apart. Sprinkle the remaining soil over the bulbs. Smooth the surface, water the bed, and mulch with chopped leaves or pine needles.

To plant scattered or single bulbs, dig a hole for each bulb with a trowel or a step-on bulb planter *(above, right)*. Mark the planter with white adhesive tape at a point 1 inch higher than the correct planting depth. Insert the planter into the earth and twist it until the tape reaches the surface. Lift the tool to pull a core of dirt out of the hole. Sprinkle in some fertilizer, mix it into the soil, then add about 1 inch of soil. Set a bulb into the hole, and replace the rest of the soil. Dampen each bulb location, and cover it with mulch or replace the turf.

4

The Finishing Touches

A garden fountain. A whimsical frog tosses a decorative arc of water toward a small garden pond. Precast in a variety of materials ranging from inexpensive plastic to costly bronze, hollow fountain figurines can be fitted with a small pump and a length of plastic tubing to add a charming focal point to any garden.

By themselves, plants can usually supply almost everything needed for a landscaped yard, from grassy lawns to tree-shaded living areas, from shrubby foundation plantings to vine-covered boundaries. But a man-made garden structure often makes a crucial addition to a landscape. Such a structure can provide a showcase for unusual plants or establish an arresting vantage point from which to take in the landscaping plan. The great estates of the past employed such elaborate devices as ornate gazebos, shimmering reflecting pools and columned loggias to dazzle and awe visitors. Large-scale flourishes of this kind are rare in present-day gardens, which tend to be laid out on a more intimate scale, but even modest efforts can produce remarkable results.

Water and rock, for example, are elements that, separately or in combination, can enhance the beauty of any yard. Important components of garden layouts for centuries, pools and fountains continue to weave their spells wherever they are used. Modestly scaled pools of concrete or plastic, set into or atop the ground, are easy to install *(pages 100-101)* and can serve as habitats for goldfish and aquatic plants while mirroring the colors of sky, trees and flowers. A small electric pump and some plastic tubing—both surprisingly easy to install—can transform a piece of hollow garden statuary into a fountain or create a miniature waterfall cascading down a rock-strewn slope *(pages 102-110)*.

Even without a waterfall, a rock garden has its uses and its beauty. It provides an answer to such problems as rock outcroppings, steep slopes or an isolated bit of ground separated by a path or driveway, for each of these sites can be converted into a rock garden, subdued or spectacular. The garden could be made up of nothing more than a blanket of English ivy, concealing or softening the jagged contours of exposed boulders. Or it might be a striking centerpiece, with a complex pattern of slopes and terraces adorned by unusual or very decorative plants.

While rock gardens command attention by lifting small plants a little way above the garden floor for better display, such structures as trellises, arbors and archways *(pages 116-121)* flaunt fast-growing vines at eye level and higher. Few garden sights can match the colorful explosion of rambler roses in full bloom on a trellis, or of a frieze of wisteria blossoms dangling from the rafters of a free-standing arbor. The simple but sturdy support structures have an added attraction in Northern gardens: They are almost as pleasing to the eye in winter, when they stand bare, as they are during the growing season, when they are largely concealed by their burdens of blossoms and foliage.

Working with Water in Pools and Fountains

For centuries landscape architects have complemented plantings with the soft reflections of a quiet pond or the dramatic arc of a fountain. Either effect can be created in a shallow, one-piece fiberglass pool, set into a hole dug to match its molded shape. A typical pool is about 6 feet long, 4 feet wide and 15 inches deep; most models come with a rounded rim, which can be blended with its surroundings by an apron of shrubs, ground covers or gravel. Pools are generally available in two colors, aqua blue and black; most landscape designers prefer black, which confers an illusion of depth.

Even the pool's actual, shallow depth, however, can present a hazard to infants and young children. Protect them with a low fence around the pool. In many communities, ordinances require such a barrier and mandate both its height and its method of construction; therefore, consult your local building authorities before planning the fence.

For a homeowner who wants the serenity of a still pond, a submerged recirculating pump placed on its side will move the water enough to keep it from stagnating, without disturbing the surface. The same pump, with slightly different plumbing, can also power a prefabricated fountain. Some fountains are simple arrangements of pipes that shoot a jet of water straight up into the air or produce a lacelike, arcing spray. Others conceal their piping in statuary, which rises from the water of the pool or stands outside the rim and sprays water inward.

The electric pump that powers a foun-tain draws in water through a screened intake to protect the mechanism from debris and discharges it through a pipe; if the fountain itself is outside the pool, the pipe is linked to it by a flexible hose. An electric cord and the hose can be draped over the edge of the pool or snaked through a hole drilled in the pool wall. For the first arrangement, spray-paint the clear plastic hose black to camouflage it; for the second, use a plastic-based clay to plug the hole around the cord and hose.

Although a pump must be small enough to remain inconspicuous in a shallow pool, it must also have enough pumping capacity to keep a fountain flowing strongly and steadily. To help determine the size of pump you need, you must know two figures: the total vertical distance, called the lift, between the outlet of the pump and the level at which water is discharged into the air; and the volume of water in your pool.

The pump you order should be able to lift that volume in a reasonable amount of time; ask the pump supplier for advice on this figure. For example, an adequate fountain pump recirculates all of the water in a 4-by-6-foot pool (about 125 gallons) in about one hour with a lift up to 5 feet. Buy a pump that delivers a little more water than necessary; the flow rate can be reduced by narrowing the outlet hose with a clamp or by crimping the end of the discharge pipe with pliers.

Bringing electricity to the pump is the trickiest part of a fountain installation. A submersible pump requires a 120-volt outdoor circuit, with a waterproof outlet box and receptacle within 6 feet of the pump. The circuit's conductor is plastic-covered underground feeder (UF) cable, usually run from a nearby junction box or from the house service panel. The receptacle must be housed in a ground-fault interrupter (GFI), an extra-sensitive circuit breaker required by electrical codes for any receptacle exposed to moisture.

Before beginning work, check to see if you will need a building-department permit to do the electrical work shown on page 102. Then check your local code for any regulations on conduit, the piping used to shield above-ground cable. You will probably have to use conduit for the circuit section in which the cable leaves the house and goes below the ground and for the one in which the cable rises to the outdoor receptacle. The code may also require that you install plastic bushings to cover the jagged ends of cut conduit. In addition, the code will dictate the depth at which the UF cable must be buried—usually 12 to 24 inches in a residential area.

With the pool installed and the pump and fountain in place, maintenance consists essentially of periodic drainage and cleaning. For drainage, let the recirculating pump do the work; simply detach the pump outlet hose from the fountain. The best way to keep pool water sweet-smelling and relatively clear (a certain amount of cloudiness is inevitable and natural) is to stock the pool with fish and aquatic plants (box, page 104), along with a population of snails and tadpoles to help maintain an ecological balance.

Installing the Pool

1 **Excavating and leveling the pit.** Dig a pit to the approximate shape and depth of the pool. Level the pit every 12 inches, using a 2-by-4 with one end set on the edge of the excavation and the other end on a scrap of wood as long as the pool is deep. Check the 2-by-4 at each point with a carpenter's level, and add or remove dirt wherever necessary. Finally, spread 1 to 2 inches of sand over the bottom of the pit, and smooth the sand evenly with a trowel or shovel.

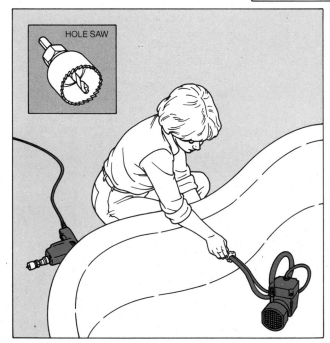

2 **Running a cord and hose into the pool.** Although the electrical cord and outlet hose of the pump can simply be draped over the side of the pool, you may prefer to conceal them. Drill a hole through the side of the pool below the water line, using a portable electric drill fitted with a 2-inch hole saw (*inset*), then place the pump on the bottom of the pool, and thread the hose and the electric cord out through the hole. Working from both sides of the pool wall, plug the hole around the cord and hose with plastic clay.

3 **Setting and filling the pool.** With a helper, lower the pool onto the sand bed, then add or remove dirt if necessary to bring the pool rim 1 to 2 inches above ground level. Fill the pool with water from a garden hose; at the same time, backfill dirt against the pool sides to equalize the pressure on the thin fiberglass walls. Finally, shovel loose soil under the outer lip of the rim.

Bringing Electricity to the Pool

1 **Fashioning an exit from the house.** Dig a narrow trench for the cable, extending it from the house to the location of the outdoor receptacle; excavate this trench to the depth required by your local building code. At the house, drill through the siding and the header joist—the horizontal board directly above the foundation wall—and install a junction box on the inside of the joist. Screw a threaded nipple—one long enough to go through the wall and into the box—to the rear of a condulet, a weatherproof fitting with a small hatch that can be opened to ease pushing cable around a bend. To the other opening in the fitting, screw a piece of conduit long enough to reach about 6 inches into the trench.

To protect the plastic electrical cable, fit a plastic bushing to the bottom of the conduit and to the open ends of all conduits and conduit fittings in the entire circuit. Push the nipple through the hole in the house wall and install a bushing on the end inside the box, then secure the conduit to the house wall with pipe clamps.

2 **Feeding cable to the inside.** After removing the cover plate and the gasket from the condulet, feed the end of a length of a UF cable from the trench up through the conduit and into the fitting. Bend the upper end of the cable to push it through the nipple and into the junction box inside the house. Then replace the gasket and cover plate of the condulet.

The cable can be linked to an existing circuit in the house or, if you prefer, you can have an electrician connect the cable directly to the main electrical panel. In either case, be sure to install a wall switch for the pump circuit at a convenient location inside the house.

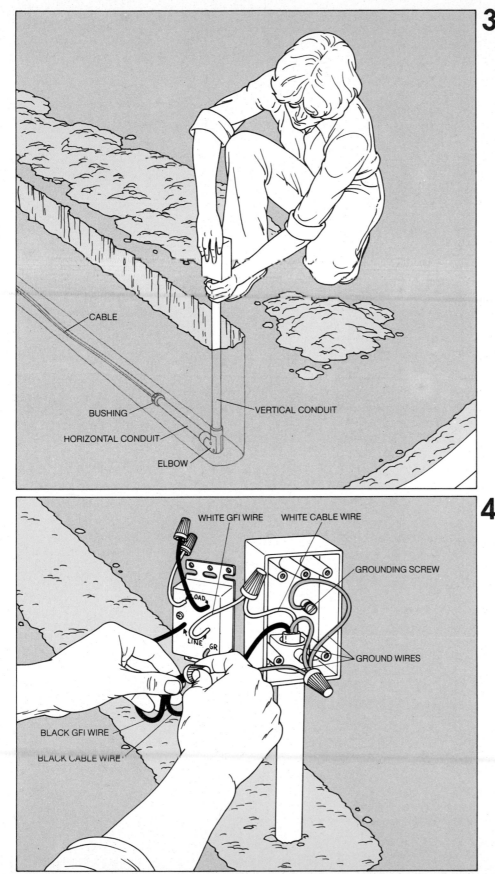

3 **Installing the outlet box.** Run the cable along the trench to the location of the outlet box, thread it through a 12-inch piece of conduit protected at one end by a bushing, and lay the conduit on the bottom of the trench. Thread an elbow connector to the end of this horizontal conduit; at the other end of the elbow, install a vertical section of conduit long enough to rise 8 inches above ground level. Screw the outlet box to the top of the vertical conduit and fill in the trench, packing soil around the vertical conduit to hold it upright.

CABLE

BUSHING

HORIZONTAL CONDUIT

ELBOW

VERTICAL CONDUIT

WHITE GFI WIRE   WHITE CABLE WIRE

GROUNDING SCREW

LOAD

LINE

GR

GROUND WIRES

BLACK GFI WIRE

BLACK CABLE WIRE

4 **Connecting a GFI.** Cap both of the GFI leads marked LOAD with wire caps. Attach a jumper wire to the grounding screw in the electrical box and, using a third wire cap, connect the jumper to the ground wires of the cable and the GFI; these wires are either bare copper or covered with green insulation. With additional wire caps, connect the black wire of the cable to the black GFI wire marked LINE, and the white cable wire to the white GFI wire marked LINE. Fold all of the wires into the outlet box, then screw the GFI in position and complete the installation with a gasket and a hinged weatherproof cover.

In Canada, check the requirements of the Canadian Electrical Code before using wire caps and jumper wires to ground the GFI. The code may require that the ground wire be looped around a bonding screw before being connected to the grounding terminal.

5 Hooking up the pump. To connect the pump to a freestanding fountain, thread and clamp the pump's outlet hose to the pipe fitting in the fountain, usually located at the back or bottom of the base. Plug the pump's electrical cord into the outdoor receptacle and use the switch in the house to start the pump.

If you prefer a simple jet or spray rather than a separate fountain, do not use an outlet hose. Instead, screw a vertical length of ½-inch threaded pipe directly to the pump outlet, and install a nozzle at the top of the pipe *(inset)*. The type of nozzle you choose will determine the shape of the jet or spray.

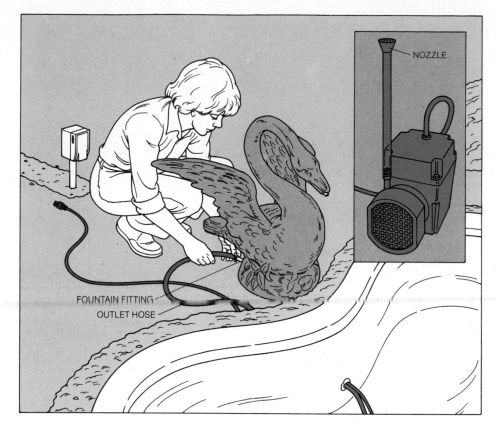

NOZZLE

FOUNTAIN FITTING
OUTLET HOSE

Aquatic Plants for a Healthy Pool

Even a shallow garden pool affords the home gardener the chance to cultivate such aquatic plants as the water hyacinth, which floats on the surface, and the hardy waterlily, which generally grows in soil packed in submerged containers. Especially suited for small pools is the pygmy lily, whose flowers are only 1 or 2 inches wide. Such plants are useful as well as decorative. A pool that contains fish should also contain plants, which release oxygen underwater and inhibit algae growth.

Techniques for planting aquatics vary. Water hyacinths can simply be tossed into the pool; they will grow roots down to the pool bottom without any help. Most waterlilies, on the other hand, must be planted in containers set on the pool bottom *(right)*. If this location submerges the young plants too deeply, prop the containers up so that no more than 3 inches of water covers the growing tips of the plants; then, as the plants send out new stems and leaves, lower the containers to the bot-

tom. Do not cover more than half the surface of a pool with leaves and flowers. A medium-sized lily will cover 8 to 10 square feet, a smaller variety 4 square feet or less.

When cold weather sets in, you can leave both plants and fish in the pool, so long as ice does not extend down to the plant roots. If the pool is shallow and winters in your area are severe, net the fish and transfer them to an indoor aquarium filled with water from the pool. Then drain the pool and move the plant containers into an unheated basement or garage. A covering of wet burlap or dampened peat moss will provide adequate moisture. When warm weather returns, clean the pool before refilling it and returning the fish and plants to their regular outdoor habitat.

Pool and plant care is minimal during the growing season. You may need to top off the pool occasionally to replace evaporated water, and you will have to trim dead leaves and flowers, and cut back rampantly spreading foliage.

How to plant a waterlily. Plant the roots of the waterlily in a container filled with 2 inches of peat moss, 9 inches of rich, clayey soil and 1 inch of pea gravel. Do not use a container made of copper, which is toxic to fish; any other material is acceptable. For most waterlilies, the ideal container size is 18 by 20 inches, but miniature varieties can thrive in 6-inch pots.

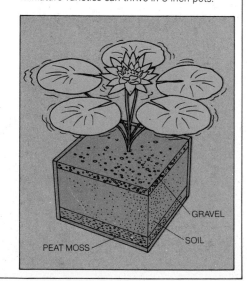

GRAVEL
SOIL
PEAT MOSS

Embellishing a Yard with a Homemade Waterfall

Much as a fireplace and a crackling fire enliven a room, a waterfall enhances a garden. The basic components of a home-built waterfall are a pond at the base of a slope, a reservoir or discharge pool at the top, a trough between the two and an electric pump that circulates water through the system. But when the parts are disguised with rough stone, and the water flows and falls, this construction has the look and sound of a scene formed by nature.

The simplest waterfall to build begins with a natural slope beside an existing garden pond. The slope, in fact, is all but essential; if your yard does not contain a pond, you can install a fiberglass pool (pages 100-104). In most other respects, the size and shape of the waterfall are limited only by your imagination. Study natural waterfalls for ideas. Consider, too, the points from which you want to view the waterfall. Then mark outlines for the trough and discharge pool on the ground with powdered chalk.

With the pool in place and the waterfall plan marked out on the ground, determine the size of pump you will need. A backyard waterfall should circulate between 100 and 400 gallons of water an hour. Measure the total height of the fall—the vertical distance from the bottom of the pool to the top of the trough—and order a pump that will lift 100 to 400 gallons per hour to that height.

The shells of the trough and discharge pool consist of premixed concrete troweled onto beds of gravel and reinforced with steel mesh. An 80-pound bag of concrete will make ½ cubic foot, enough to cover about 1½ square feet when spread four inches thick. To determine the areas of the shells, measure the trough and the discharge pool separately, then add 10 per cent to allow for the extra area created by the pool's depth.

Both of the concrete shells are painted with a thin layer of masonry bonding agent, then coated with a one-inch-thick layer of black waterproof mortar; the mortar not only makes the surfaces leakproof, but serves as a bed for the decorative stones. You will need enough mortar to cover the entire surface of the trough and pool, and an additional quantity to bond the stones in place. One cubic foot of mortar spread an inch thick covers 12 square feet.

Mix the concrete and the mortar separately in a mortar pan, stirring with a shovel. To mix the concrete, pour a bag of premixed concrete into the pan and add just enough water so that a handful will barely hold together in a clump. To make a cubic foot of mortar, mix 100 pounds of fine builder's sand with 16 pounds of portland cement and 18 ounces of black cement pigment (sometimes called carbon black), then add enough water to make a stiff mixture that will stick to a trowel held upside down.

Stone for the fall itself and for the camouflage of the concrete shell can be harvested anywhere you find it. Or you may purchase it from a quarry; many quarries will also deliver the stone to the site, but you can cut costs by transporting it yourself. Handle all stone carefully to prevent nicks and breaks that can spoil the weathered appearance.

Premixed concrete, portland cement, cement pigment, wire reinforcing mesh, masonry bonding agent, gravel and builder's sand are all available from masonry suppliers. You will need a few specialized tools: a mason's trowel, a float and a tuck pointer. If you must cut stones to fit, you will also need a mason's chisel and the short-handled mallet called a maul. Always wear heavy gloves and steel-toed work boots when working with concrete, mortar or stone and, if you cut stones, wear safety goggles.

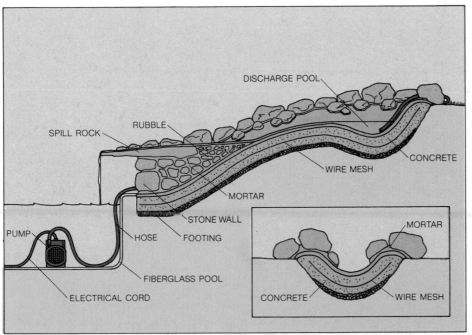

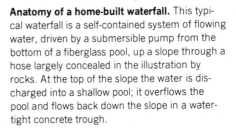

Anatomy of a home-built waterfall. This typical waterfall is a self-contained system of flowing water, driven by a submersible pump from the bottom of a fiberglass pool, up a slope through a hose largely concealed in the illustration by rocks. At the top of the slope the water is discharged into a shallow pool; it overflows the pool and flows back down the slope in a watertight concrete trough.

A cross-section view (inset) shows the construction of the trough. It consists of a 4-inch-thick concrete shell resting on a 1-inch-deep bed of gravel and reinforced by 10-gauge steel wire mesh. It is coated with a 1-inch layer of waterproof mortar. The trough channels water to the fall—which consists of a stone wall backed up with rubble, and a flat spill rock. Water pours over the lip of the spill rock, which is cantilevered 5 inches over the edge of the lower pool. The rims and surfaces of both the trough and the discharge pool are camouflaged by rocks and pebbles, all set in a bed of waterproof mortar.

Building the Concrete Shells

1 Digging the trough and the pool. Mark the outlines of the trough and the discharge pool with powdered chalk sprinkled on the ground. At the side of the fiberglass pool, and within the boundary lines, dig the fall's footing, consisting of a 5-inch-deep, level excavation extending 8 inches from the pool's edge; shovel the excavated soil onto a piece of canvas or into a wheelbarrow for later removal. Then, working up the slope from the footing, dig a trench with gently sloping sides to the planned depth of the stream plus 5 inches for the concrete shell and its mortar coating. At the top of the slope, dig the discharge pool to the same depth as the trench and with similarly sloping sides. Finally, pour a 1-inch-deep layer of gravel into the trough and the discharge pool.

BOUNDARY LINE

FIBERGLASS POOL

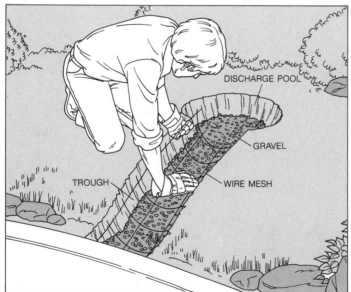

DISCHARGE POOL

GRAVEL

WIRE MESH

TROUGH

2 Laying wire reinforcement. Measure the sides and bottom of the trough with a flexible measuring tape, cut a section of reinforcing steel mesh to fit, and press the mesh into the trough, shaping it to the contours of the excavation. Similarly, cut and shape a section of mesh to fit the discharge pool.

Set pieces of brick or stone beneath the mesh to raise it 2 inches above the gravel bed. Mix the concrete and water in a mortar pan.

3 Building the footing. Trowel concrete into the excavated area beside the fiberglass pool as a footing for the stones of the fall. Build the footing 4 inches thick; check the depth by running the end of a mason's rule down through the concrete to the gravel bed below.

4 Shaping the concrete shells. Working in sections 2 to 3 feet long, trowel a 4-inch layer of concrete onto the bottom and sides of the trough *(left)*; at the rims of the excavation, build the concrete up to about an inch above the level of the ground outside of the trough. Trowel a concrete shell for the discharge pool in the same way. Using your gloved hands, shape the concrete rims of the trough and pool into a single, continous rounded lip *(right)*. Then use the tip of the trowel to smooth out any irregularities on the surface of the concrete.

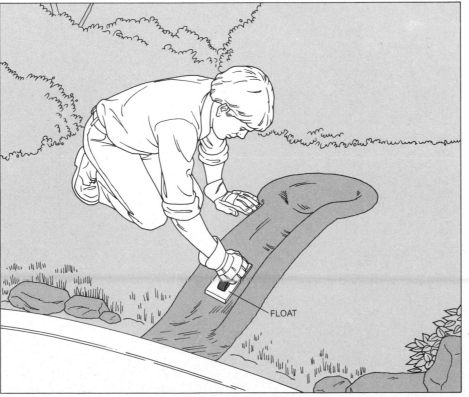

5 Finishing the surface. Skim a wood float over the concrete, pressing down just enough to smooth the surface. Begin at the centers of the trough and the pool and work up the sides, compacting the concrete and pushing out all the water that rises to the surface.

107

Adding the Stonework

1 Applying a waterproof base. Using a 3-inch-wide disposable paintbrush, spread a coat of masonry bonding agent over the surface of the trough and the discharge pool. Let the bonding agent dry until it is tacky to the touch.

Mix a batch of dark-colored waterproof mortar in a mortar pan and, using a mason's trowel, coat the trough and pool with a 1-inch layer of mortar. Let the mortar cure for at least three hours.

While the mortar is curing, set the stones you will use for the waterfall on the ground, with their good sides up, so that you can find the right stone for the right place at a glance.

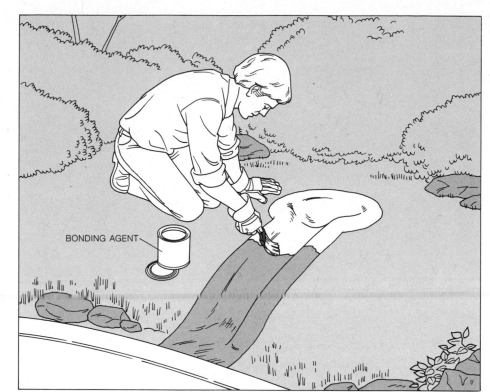

BONDING AGENT

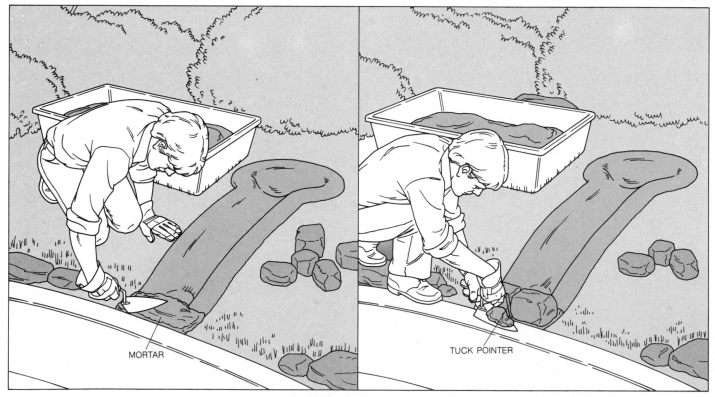

MORTAR

TUCK POINTER

2 Building the fall. From a second batch of mortar, trowel a 1-inch mortar bed on the concrete footing *(left)*. Select a large, flat-bottomed stone, paint its base with bonding agent and set the stone firmly in the mortar bed. Trim away excess mortar with the trowel. Set a second large stone beside the first, leaving a ½-inch gap between the two; fill the gap with mortar, using the trowel as a palette and pushing mortar from it with a tuck pointer *(right)*, until the mortar is compacted tightly between the stones. Lay a ½-inch bed of mortar on top of the two stones. Coat the base of another flat-bottomed stone with bonding agent and set it in the mor-tar, overlapping the joint between the bottom stones; set two more stones on either side to complete the course. Lay successive courses of stone to build the wall up to the desired height. Note: The stones should be fairly uniform in shape; if necessary, use a stone chisel and maul to chip off irregularities.

3 **Laying a base for the rubble.** Spread a 1-inch bed of waterproof mortar on the trough, starting just behind the stone wall and extending up to a point level with the top of the wall. To find this point, set a level on the wall with one end touching the bottom of the trough. Slide the level up or down the slope of the trough until the bubble is centered in the glass tube of the level.

4 **Backfilling with rubble.** Select enough small and medium-sized stones to fill the area behind the wall. Paint the base of each stone with bonding agent and set it in the mortar bed, separating the stones by about ½ inch on all sides. Trowel mortar into the spaces between stones and compact it with a tuck pointer.

Spread another ½-inch coat of mortar on top of the rubble and set in more stones. Continue this procedure until you have built up a flat surface of rubble and mortar extending back into the trough and level with the top of the wall.

RUBBLE

STONE WALL

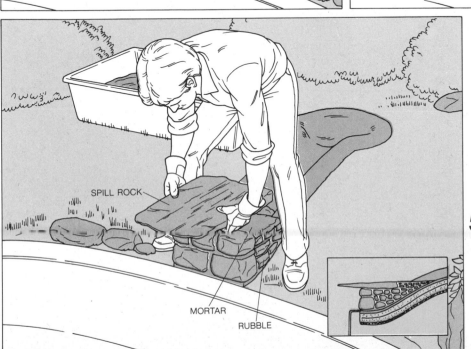

SPILL ROCK

MORTAR

RUBBLE

5 **Setting the spill rock.** Spread a ½-inch bed of mortar over the top of the stone wall and the rubble fill. Set the spill rock in the mortar, with one edge of the rock cantilevered out over the edge of the wall to project at least 5 inches over the edge of the fiberglass pool. Fill the area just behind the spill rock with mortar and small chunks of rubble, then coat the top of this rubble with mortar to form a smooth, even surface that is level with the top of the spill rock *(inset)*.

6 Completing the stonework. Line the opposite edges of the spill rock with stones, forming two low walls to direct water straight over the fall. For this part of the job, paint the base of each stone with bonding agent, set it in its own mortar bed and fill in the joints *(page 108, Step 2)*.

Continue setting stones along the edges of the trough and, if you wish, set small stones in the trough, working your way up the slope; set the final stones on the bottom and around the rim of the discharge pool.

7 Raking the joints. After the mortar has set for 30 to 40 minutes, use a tuck pointer to rake out the joints between stones and around the base of each stone. Rake out mortar until the joints are barely visible, but leave enough to hold the stones securely. Clean off any spatters of mortar with a wet stiff-bristled brush. Install the pump, pump wiring and plumbing *(pages 100-104)*, and fill the upper and lower pools.

Rock Gardens: Rugged Frames for Alpine Displays

An ordinary garden is a sort of botanical still life, often elegantly artificial. By contrast, a rock garden is a wilderness area in miniature. Like a landscape painter, a rock gardener achieves a natural effect by subtly recasting nature, placing rocks and tiny plants to simulate a mountain landscape. On a steep slope a rock garden has the practical virtue of substituting for grass, but even on a flat site a raised-bed rock garden *(pages 113-114)* can be an intriguing miniature meadow.

Careful planning is particularly important, because both rocks and the so-called alpine plants typical of rock gardens are difficult to reinstall. Sketch an overall design on graph paper, then test its visual effect by staking out the rock locations with sheets of newspaper. Exploit your yard's natural topography by building the garden around any existing rock outcrops. Since alpine plants require particularly good drainage, they are generally planted on steep slopes; drainage is further improved by a planting base of porous rubble topped by a sandy soil mixture. Most species require sunlight but do not tolerate a baking heat. If possible, orient the garden for an eastern or northern exposure; alternatively, a stand of trees can filter light without throwing the garden into deep shade.

Because the garden's rocky skeleton should look natural and unobtrusive, it is best to choose a single type of local, neutral-colored stone, porous enough to retain moisture. Most often used are sandstone and gray limestone, which is ubiquitous and inexpensive but has one drawback: Acid-loving plants must be planted above it on a slope, because the alkaline lime sometimes leaches into the soil below. Other possibilities include gneiss, shale, schist and tufa.

The best source of rocks is a local quarry. You can have stone delivered by the hundredweight or by the ton, but a bulk load will contain many unusable rocks; it is usually better to haul away picked stones from the quarry yourself, or to pick stones for later delivery.

For the most part, avoid small rocks, which tend to clutter a garden; also avoid rounded stones, which often look artificial. Look for a few big, irregular rocks of the desired shape—flat ones for a ledge or a wall, boulders for an isolated outcrop. By using the techniques explained on pages 22-24, two people can safely handle fairly large stones; those weighing several hundred pounds must be placed in a prepared bed *(page 112)* by a quarry operator with a crane.

Before you actually start digging holes and placing stones, schedule the job to suit your capabilities. A garden less than 6 feet square generally can be built and planted in two or three weekends, but a larger one may be best assembled piecemeal. The step-by-step approach is particularly important in a raised-bed garden, where plants are set in during construction rather than afterward.

The traditional plants for a rock garden are dwarf alpine species that grow above the tree line, but many gardeners now substitute hybrid cousins that flourish nearer to sea level. The garden's mainstays are exuberant clusters of tiny wildflowers, available from garden shops and by mail order. The tiny scale of the plantings and the garden's lean soil exclude most sea-level flowers, but a few other lowland plants such as herbs, succulents and dwarf shrubs fit naturally into a rocky setting. Once planted and topped with gravel, the garden needs little care. It requires only weeding, the control of snails and slugs, and an occasional watering if the leaves begin to wilt during a drought.

An understated alpine habitat. Rocks are a natural, unobtrusive setting for this garden's true centerpiece, an array of tiny alpine plants. An artful, apparently random design mimics natural rock formations, with large, deeply embedded rocks that suggest ledges and outcrops.

Specimens are planted in their natural locations—succulents in crevices, for example, and trailing flowers on ledges—but the plant placement also reflects the desired visual effect. Because most alpine plants are less than 8 inches tall, dwarf trees are not planted in their natural location at the bottom of a slope when they might block the view. Plants of a single species are grouped together to avoid clutter and heighten visual contrasts. Placement also anticipates each plant's growth cycle, so that the garden remains visually balanced as flowers and foliage change with the seasons *(page 115)*.

TRAILING FLOWERS

DWARF CONIFER

SUCCULENTS

Building a Rock Garden on a Slope

1 Preparing the drainage bed. Using a spade, strip all sod off a section of the slope up to 6 feet square, then dig up about 18 inches of soil from the section. Reserve the sod and soil in separate piles for later use.

To provide proper drainage, fill the bottom of the section with 6 inches of broken bricks or rocks. Cover this rubble with pieces of the original sod, grass side down, or with stone chips or coarse sand; such materials prevent soil from clogging the drainage bed.

2 Preparing the soil. If your soil is particularly unstable, support the rocks that will project above the soil by setting flat, 4-inch-thick rocks 1 to 2 feet apart on the drainage bed. Mix two parts of coarse sand with one part each of topsoil, leaf mold and fine gravel. Fill the excavation with the mixture, completely burying the flat rocks, and rake the surface level with the surrounding grade. Thoroughly wet the bed with a hose and let the dirt settle for a week or so, then fill any low spots with more of the soil mixture.

RUBBLE

SOD

Arranging Rocks in Formation

Planting rocks in a slope. For each rock, dig a step in the slope deep enough to accommodate at least one third of the rock's bulk; shape the step so that the rock's broadest side will face down and its top will tilt into the slope, draining water back into the soil. Pack soil firmly around the rock, then stand on the rock and shift your weight to test its stability; if you feel any movement, embed the rock more deeply. Plant the biggest rocks first, working from the bottom of the slope to the top; then sparingly plant a few small rocks in the same way.

Building a rock outcrop. Select several thick, flat rocks with similar lines of horizontal strata and vertical fractures. Plant the bottom rock, tilting its top into the slope; the angle can vary from slight to extreme according to the garden's design. Cover the top of the rock with about ¾ inch of soil mixture; then, one by one, dig steps for succeeding rocks and stack them above and behind the first, securely embedding each in the slope and topping it with a very thin layer of loose soil. Align the strata and fracture lines wherever possible; if necessary, adjust a rock's angle by inserting chips of stone beneath it. Hose away dirt from the exposed faces of the rocks, then trowel soil into the crevices and plant them with specimens that thrive in dry soil.

STRATA LINES

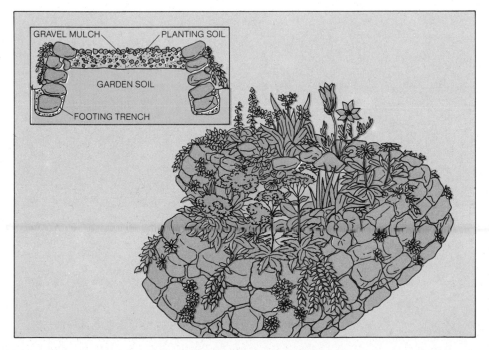

GRAVEL MULCH PLANTING SOIL

GARDEN SOIL

FOOTING TRENCH

A Rock Garden for a Level Site

Anatomy of a raised-bed garden. Although rock gardens are traditionally built on slopes, a similar effect can be achieved on level ground by constructing stone walls that raise a garden bed 2 or 3 feet above the ground, ensuring proper drainage. Built up over shallow footing trenches (*inset*), the mortarless walls slope inward for stability; crevices between stones are packed with soil and plants. The basin formed by the wall often is filled with earth, topped by a deep bed of planting soil and 2 inches of gravel; a planter less than 2 feet deep often is entirely filled with planting soil. Together the walls and bed create an effective setting for a selection of alpine plants (*chart, page 115*).

Building a Walled Garden Bed

1 **Laying the foundation.** Mark the wall's outer boundary with stakes and string. Just inside the string, dig a footing trench 6 to 12 inches deep and slightly wider than the largest stone slabs. Lower these slabs into the trench, tilting each slightly inward and butting the stones snugly together so that their tops form a smooth shelf. Pack earth around this course of stones and cover it with ½ inch of an alpine planting mixture—two parts of coarse sand and one part each of garden topsoil, leaf mold and fine gravel.

2 **Building the walls.** Lay subsequent courses of square rocks, staggering the vertical joints to prevent erosion and setting each course slightly within the one below it. As the wall rises above the ground, check its inward slope with a homemade slope gauge. To make the gauge, nail scraps of 1-by-2 into a right triangle, consisting of a short horizontal side, a long vertical side, and a longer diagonal; the horizontal side should measure about 2 inches for every foot of the vertical one. When a level shows that the vertical side is plumb, or perfectly vertical, the diagonal side will be at the correct angle for the wall.

Compensate for uneven or wobbly rocks by using thicker layers of soil and by inserting chips of stone. Set plants at intervals in the crevices. If your soil drains poorly, line the basin inside the wall with gravel; reinforce weak sections of the wall by bracing boulders against its inner face. Periodically, fill the basin inside the wall with earth and tamp it firmly against the wall; use planting mixture for the top 10 inches of the bed. After rooting seedlings in the bed, cover the exposed soil with 2 inches of gravel mulch.

SLOPE GAUGE

A Selection of Rock-garden Plants

	Zones	Soil		Light			Height			Growth habit			Special traits			Flower color			
		Acid	Alkaline	Shade	Partial shade	Full sun	Under 6 in.	6-12 in.	Over 12 in.	Upright	Spreading	Trailing	Flowers	Foliage	Evergreen	White-green	Yellow-orange	Pink-red	Blue-purple
PLANTS SUITABLE FOR ROCK GARDEN																			
Anemone, European wood (ANEMONE NEMOROSA)	3-8	●			●	●		●			●		●			●		●	●
Basket-of-gold (AURINIA SAXATILIS)	4		●			●		●			●		●				●		
Bishop's hat (EPIMEDIUM GRANDIFLORUM)	3-8			●			●	●			●		●	●		●	●	●	●
Bleeding heart, fringed (DICENTRA EXIMIA)	3-8	●		●				●	●		●		●	●		●		●	
Candytuft, evergreen (IBERIS SEMPERVIRENS)	3-10		●		●		●			●	●		●			●			
Cheddar plant (DIANTHUS GRATIANOPOLITANUS)	4				●		●				●		●			●			
Foam flower (TIARELLA CORDIFOLIA)	4	●		●			●				●		●			●			
Goldenstar (CHRYSOGONUM VIRGINIANUM)	4-8	●		●			●		●	●	●		●				●		
Harebell, Carpathian (CAMPANULA CARPATICA)	3-8				●		●			●			●			●			●
Iris, dwarf bearded (IRIS PUMILA)	5		●			●		●		●			●			●	●	●	●
Iris, dwarf crested (IRIS CRISTATA)	3-8	●			●		●			●			●			●			●
Leadwort (CERATOSTIGMA PLUMBAGINOIDES)	6-10				●	●				●		●	●	●					●
Phlox, wild blue (PHLOX DIVARICATA)	4	●			●		●			●			●			●			●
Pink, moss (PHLOX SUBULATA)	3-8				●	●	●				●		●			●		●	●
Pink, wild (SILENE CAROLINIANA)	6			●			●		●		●		●					●	
Primrose, Siebold (PRIMULA SIEBOLDII)	5	●		●			●			●			●			●		●	
Rose, sun (HELIANTHEMUM NUMMULARIUM)	5-9		●		●		●		●	●	●		●			●	●	●	
Sandwort, mountain (ARENARIA MONTANA)	4-10	●			●	●					●	●	●			●			
Soapwort, rock (SAPONARIA OCYMOIDES)	2-8				●		●				●	●	●			●		●	
Thrift, common (ARMERIA MARITIMA)	4-8				●	●	●			●			●	●	●	●		●	
PLANTS SUITABLE FOR A RAISED BED																			
Alpencress (HUTCHINSIA ALPINA)	4-8				●		●			●		●	●	●		●			
Anemone, rue (ANEMONELLA THALICTROIDES)	3-6	●			●			●		●			●			●		●	
Avens, mountain (DRYAS OCTOPETALA)	2-8				●	●	●				●	●	●	●	●	●			
Babies'-breath, creeping (GYPSOPHILA REPENS 'FRATENSIS')	3-8		●		●	●	●				●	●	●					●	
Bellflower, Dalmatian (CAMPANULA PORTENSCHLAGIANA)	5		●		●	●			●			●	●						●
Columbine, alpinerock (AQUILEGIA BERTOLONII)	6-7			●		●		●		●			●						●
Fleabane (ERIGERON AUREUS)	5-9			●	●		●			●			●				●		
Gentian, stemless (GENTIANA ACAULIS)	3-8		●		●		●				●		●			●			●
Hepatica (HEPATICA AMERICANA)	3-8			●		●				●			●			●		●	●
Iris, Alba (IRIS GRACILIPES)	6-7	●			●		●			●			●						●
Jasmine, rock (ANDROSACE SARMENTOSA)	3-7				●	●	●				●		●	●				●	
Lewisia cotyledon (LEWISIA COTYLEDON)	5-7			●			●	●		●			●		●	●		●	
Pink, alpine (DIANTHUS ALPINUS)	2-4		●		●	●	●				●		●			●		●	
Pink, sea (ARMERIA JUNIPERIFOLIA)	4-8		●		●	●	●				●		●	●	●	●		●	
Primrose, bird's eye (PRIMULA JULIAN)	3-8			●			●			●			●			●	●	●	●
Rockfoil (SAXIFRAGA PANICULATA)	2-3		●	●			●	●			●		●		●	●			
Rose, Warley (AETHIONEMA X WARLEYENSE)	6-7		●		●	●		●			●		●	●	●			●	
Verna Nana (VERNA NANA)	4-8				●	●	●				●		●			●			
Violet, dog-toothed (ERYTHRONIUM DENS-CANIS)	3-9	●			●			●		●			●			●		●	●
Whitlow grass (DRABA AIZOIDES)	6		●		●	●	●			●			●				●		

Choosing plants for rock gardens. The top half of this chart lists plants suitable for a rock garden; the bottom half, plants recommended for raised beds. In both sections, plants are listed by their most common English names, followed by their scientific Latin names. The first column indicates the climatic zone or zones in which each plant can be grown, keyed by number to the map on page 122. Dots in the columns for Soil and Light indicate the best growing conditions for each plant; the absence of a dot in the Soil column means that a plant can thrive in either type of soil. Heights given include the height of flowers, if any. Dots in the columns for Growth Habit, Flower Color and Special Habits indicate other significant physical features; multiple dots in any of these columns mean that the features vary within a species.

Trellises and Arbors for Climbing Plants

If left to grow untrained, most vines will ramble aimlessly across the ground, over fences and up walls. They look better and are easier to care for when they are deliberately grown for display on trellises, arbors and archways. Such structures can also enhance attractive features of the landscape, such as patios and garden paths, or conceal unattractive elements, such as toolsheds and trash bins.

The simplest support for garden vines is a trellis, upon which a climbing plant can be trained to grow vertically and horizontally. Trellises come in many sizes and shapes, from lightweight structures of thin wood strips called laths to massive frames and bulky grids for such heavy vines as grape and wisteria. The trellises can be erected singly or in series against a wall, at right angles to a fence or doorway, or as freestanding yard dividers or centerpieces.

A trellis mounted horizontally on a set of posts becomes an arbor *(pages 118-119)*, providing a pleasant, sundappled shelter; the sides can be enclosed with vertical trellises or left completely open to sun and breeze. A pair of vertical trellises joined by a graceful arch *(pages 119-121)* becomes an elegant gateway; a series of arches over a path is sometimes called a pergola.

Designing and building a trellis, arbor or archway need not be difficult or complicated. A few basic construction rules ensure that the structure will be sufficiently sturdy and well anchored to support a full-grown vine and withstand high winds or frost heaves.

Wall-mounted trellises should be built with frames or spacers that hold the plants at least 2 inches away from the wall. This clearance permits air to circulate behind the trellis and prevents a vine from touching the wall surface, where its moisture can rot wood and blister paint.

To support freestanding trellises, arbors and archways, set sturdy posts 2 to 3 feet deep. It is usually not necessary to anchor the posts in concrete; just tamp the soil around the posts firmly. For especially heavy structures, however, add a 1-foot layer of dry cement at the bottom of each posthole for extra stability.

Trellises and other vine supports can be made from a wide variety of materials, from plumbing pipes to galvanized steel wire and plastic rope; the traditional and most common material is wood. Naturally weather-resistant woods, such as redwood and cedar, are the most attractive and expensive. Less costly are softwoods, such as pine and fir, pressure-treated, stained or painted to resist rot. Wood that touches or enters the ground—the support posts of a freestanding trellis, for example—should be further protected with a coating of nontoxic wood preservative, such as copper naphthenate.

Building a trellis can generally be done with just a few basic tools: A saw and a hammer or staple gun usually will suffice. Hardware for joinery is inexpensive and readily available; use galvanized-steel or aluminum nails, staples, hinges and other metal parts, to avoid unsightly rust stains.

Nearly all vines will grow well on a trellis or arbor if the soil at the base is moderately moist but well drained. A few vines, notably Boston ivy, may be adversely affected by the alkalinity of lime seeping from a nearby concrete or concrete-block foundation; either correct the soil with annual additions of sulfur compounds *(page 32)* or substitute such alkaline-tolerant plants as clematis.

As young vines begin to climb a trellis, tie the stems loosely to the supports with soft, moisture-resistant material, such as raffia, garden cord or even strips cut from discarded nylon hose. Secure plants from the base upward, and check periodically to make sure the ties are not restricting plant growth. As perennial vines mature and fasten themselves securely to the supports, the ties can be discarded.

A Sampler of Trellises

A hinged trellis. Vertical and horizontal 1-by-2 slats, nailed together in a grid pattern, are mounted on 2-by-4 posts to provide support for heavy, bulky vines. Spacers and sets of hooks and eyes hold the trellis 6 inches from the house wall; a pair of strap hinges, fitted into the posts *(inset)*, permit the entire structure to be folded down when the wall must be cleaned or painted.

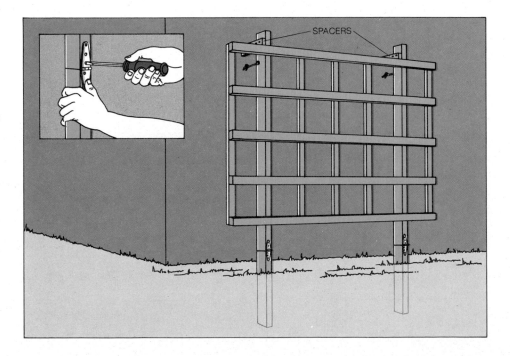

SPACERS

A basket-weave trellis. In a trellis especially suitable for light vines, thin, 2-inch-wide slats are woven together and nailed to a frame of 2-by-2 boards. To create the basket-weave pattern of slats, nail the tops of the vertical slats to the frame, at least 3 inches apart, then weave the horizontal slats through the vertical slats *(inset)*, working each one upward to form a row of open squares. As you set each horizontal slat into position, nail its ends to the frame; when you have positioned the last horizontal slat, nail the bottoms of the vertical slats to the frame. Finally, nail the frame to 2-by-4 posts in front of a wall or, as shown here, as a freestanding unit.

A latticework trellis. The diamond-shaped pattern of this latticework trellis can be assembled with strips of narrow lath for lightweight vines or with thicker, stronger slats for heavy plants. To simplify laying out the crisscross strips, use one strip as a spacing device *(inset)*. Staple or nail the ends of the strips to a 2-by-2 frame, then trim the parts of strips projecting beyond the frame with a saber or circular saw, and nail the entire trellis to a wall or to posts.

A wing trellis. Set at right angles to a fence or wall, a wing trellis serves as an informal space divider. The trellises shown here consist of vertical 1-by-1 boards (called stop bead at building-supply stores) nailed to three-sided 2-by-4 frames. The horizontal members of the frames are fastened to a fence by pairs of galvanized corner plates *(inset)*; the vertical posts simply rest on the ground and require no posthole digging.

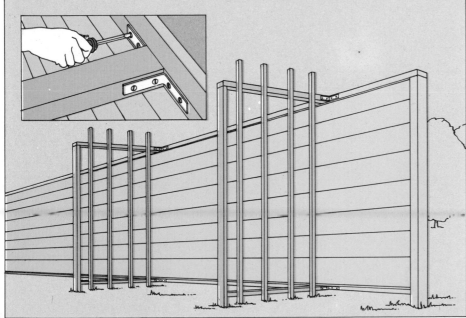
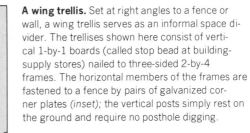

Espaliers: Touches of Whimsy for the Garden

Normally, trellises are not needed to support a bush or a tree, but they can be used to impart whimsical, two-dimensional shapes to such nonclimbing plants as fruit trees, flowering dogwood and forsythia. The creation of such displays as the candelabrum at right is part of an ancient art form called espalier, which attained widespread popularity in the highly stylized formal gardens of 18th Century Europe.

Trellises for espaliers are generally wall-mounted rather than freestanding,

with horizontal slats beginning about 18 inches above the ground and spaced 12 to 16 inches apart. Vertical slats are unnecessary: Upward-growing stems support themselves and need no restraint.

When planting, position the tree or bush directly under the center of the espalier trellis and prune the main stem back 2 to 4 inches below the bottom slat. As the plant grows, tie its lateral shoots to the slats to force horizontal growth; cut off any shoots that cannot be trained to the desired pattern.

Building a Post-and-beam Arbor

1 Setting the posts. With a spade or a posthole digger, dig four holes up to 8 feet apart for the 4-by-4 posts of the arbor. Make each hole about 18 inches wide and 3 feet deep; if the ground is soft, place a flat rock at the bottom of the hole. Set each post into its hole and align it with the planned building line. As a helper holds each post upright and checks with a level to make sure that it is vertical, firmly tamp soil a few inches at a time around the base of the post with a tamping tool or a length of 2-by-4. To keep the posts plumb until construction is completed, nail two temporary 2-by-4 braces at least 5 feet long to adjoining surfaces of each post; anchor these braces to short stakes driven into the ground.

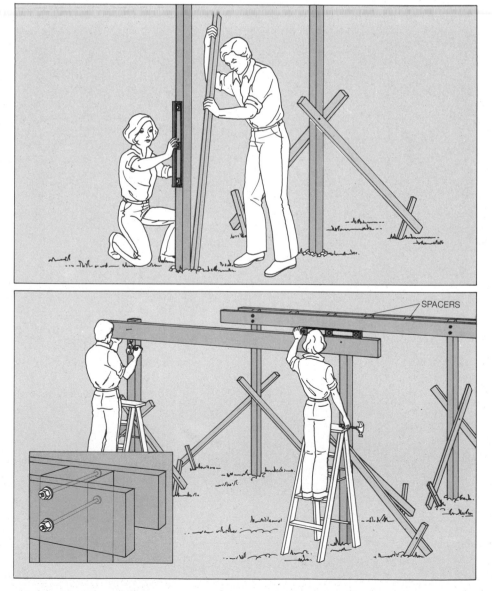

SPACERS

2 Mounting the beams. Cut two pairs of beams from 1-by-8 boards, allowing for an overhang of at least 1 foot at both ends of the arbor. With the aid of a helper, raise each beam to the top of the posts, level the beam and nail it temporarily to the posts. After each pair of beams has been leveled and nailed to the opposite sides of a pair of posts, drill two ½-inch holes through the beams and each post. Run 6-inch carriage bolts through these holes, and secure the bolts with washers and nuts (inset). Cut spacers 4 to 6 inches long from scraps of post lumber; nail them between the double beams, flush with the top edges, at intervals of 12 to 18 inches.

3 **Installing the rafters.** Measure and mark rafter positions on the tops of the beams at equal intervals up to 24 inches. Cut rafters from 1-by-6 boards, allowing for at least a foot of overhang on both sides of the arbor. Position each rafter edgewise on its marks, and toenail it to the beams from both sides. If toenailing is difficult, secure the rafters to the beams with metal rafter anchors (*inset*), obtainable at building-supply stores.

An Optional Eggcrate Grid

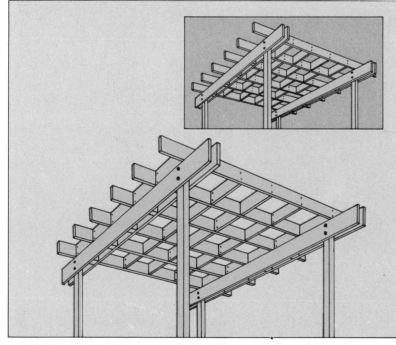

Filling the spaces between rafters. To brace the rafters of an arbor against twisting under a load of heavy vines, and to increase the shade provided by the arbor, create a grid with 1-by-6 spacer boards set crosswise between the rafters. Mark the rafters for spacers at regular intervals from the inner beam on one side of the arbor to the inner beam on the other, then install one set of spacers between every other pair of rafters, nailing directly through the rafters into the ends of the spacers; toenail the remaining spacers to the faces of the rafters. Alternatively, stagger the spacers in a pattern (*inset*) that makes toenailing unnecessary.

Building an Arch of Trellises

1 **Putting up the support posts.** Mark positions for front posts 2 to 3 feet apart if you plan to install a gate, 2 to 5 feet apart otherwise; position the rear posts 2 to 4 feet behind the front ones. Put up all four posts (*opposite, Step 1*), using 4-by-4 timbers that rise at least 6 feet above the ground. Allow about an inch of play at the top of each post, and do not use braces. At intervals of 8 to 12 inches, nail 1-by-2 strips crosswise up the sides of the archway.

2 **Making an arch template.** On a sheet of cardboard, draw a horizontal line equal to the distance between the outside edges of the posts. At each end of the line, measure in 3½ inches (the actual width of 4-by-4 posts); indicate these points with short vertical marks. Nail or pin one end of a length of string to the center of the line, tie the other end of the string around a pencil and, with the string held taut, draw one semicircular arc between the ends of the line and another between the vertical marks. Cut out the arch template with a utility knife.

3 **Cutting out the arches.** Arrange three 1-by-8 boards into a rough arch on which you can lay the entire template; set a long board at the top, resting upon the two side boards. Scribe and cut the side boards along the lines at which they meet the long board, so that the three pieces abut each other. Trace the arch on the boards and cut it out with a saber saw. Assemble and cut three more sets of boards in the same way.

Cut four more arches with the same template. For this set of arches, place long boards at the sides of the arch (inset), rather than the top, so that the joints will be staggered when all of the arch segments are assembled.

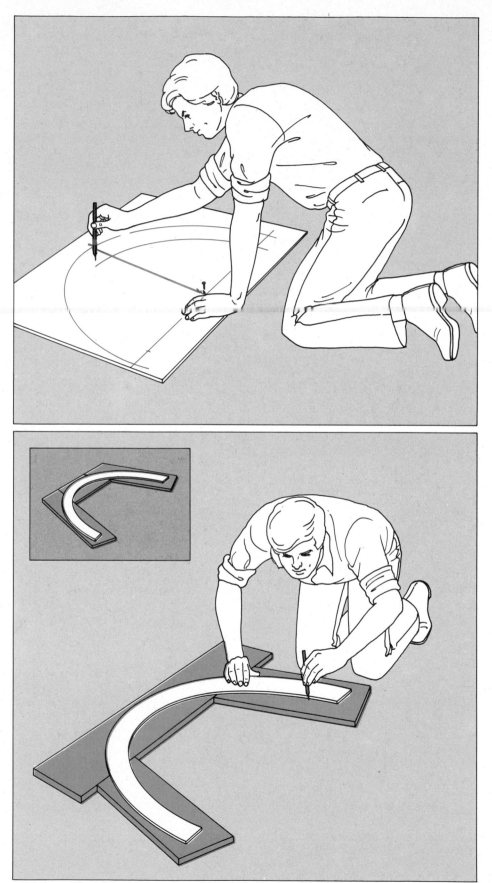

4 **Building two-layer arches.** Align a pair of arches—one from each set, so that the joints are staggered—and fasten them together with construction adhesive and 1¼-inch nails. Repeat this procedure three more times so that you end up with 4 two-layer arches.

5 **Assembling four-layer arches.** Align two double-thick arches so that adjoining layers do not have the same joint pattern, and fasten these four-layer arches with adhesive and 2½-inch nails. Trim and smooth the curved surfaces and the flat ends with a rasp or a forming tool.

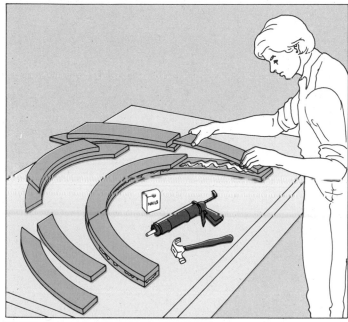

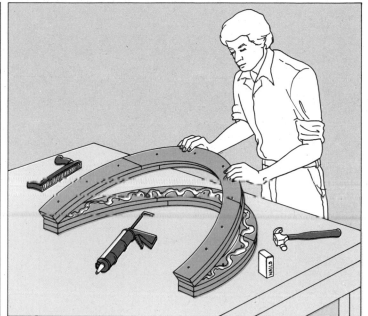

6 **Setting the arches.** With a helper, lift the front arch onto the posts, align the front face of the arch flush to the front of the posts and toe-nail the arch to the post. Similarly, mount the rear arch flush with the back of the rear posts. Nail 1-by-2 boards between the arches at the intervals established for the posts (Step 1), and tamp the earth firmly at the base of the posts.

To build a pergola over a garden path, erect a series of identical arches 2 to 3 feet apart.

A Map of Winter Temperatures

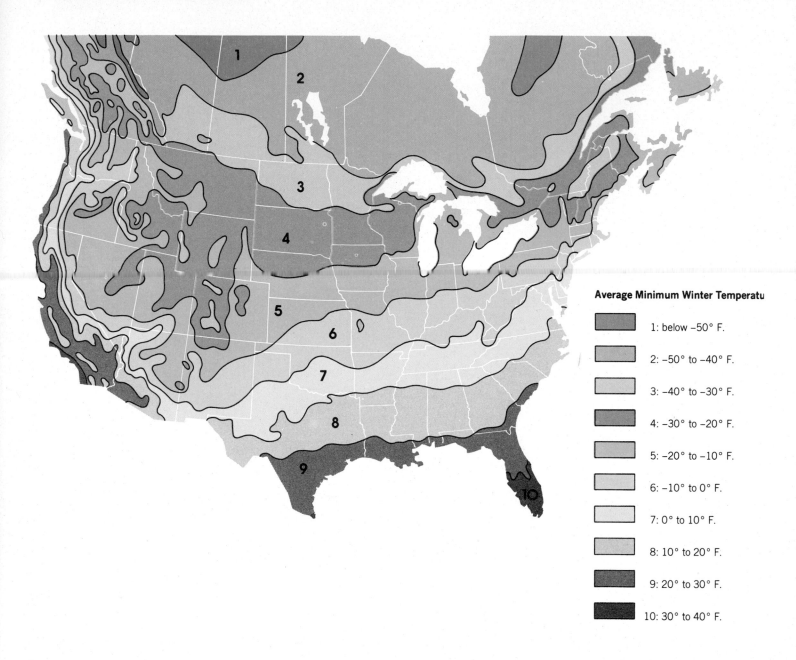

Average Minimum Winter Temperatu

1: below −50° F.

2: −50° to −40° F.

3: −40° to −30° F.

4: −30° to −20° F.

5: −20° to −10° F.

6: −10° to 0° F.

7: 0° to 10° F.

8: 10° to 20° F.

9: 20° to 30° F.

10: 30° to 40° F.

Plants and winter cold. Successful landscaping depends upon a choice of plants that thrive on the land they adorn. Normally—and, to some, surprisingly—a main basis of the selection is not so much local soil conditions and moisture (which can be altered artificially) as the severity of winter cold that the plants must endure. This map, based on weather data, divides North America into 10 numbered and colored zones, each distinguished by an average minimum winter temperature. The zones have been adopted by many authorities, including the U.S. Department of Agriculture, to classify plants according to the regions in which they flourish. In this book, charts of ground covers (*page 61*), vines (*page 63*), flowering shrubs (*pages 94-95*) and rock-garden plants (*page 115*) are keyed to the map. Use these charts and the map together to select plants that will grow best in your area. Three charts—on grass (*page 54*), trees (*pages 82-83*) and evergreen shrubs (*page 95*)—are keyed to maps in the body of the book; for these plant types, temperature has less influence on growth than rainfall and soil type.

A Map of Final Frosts

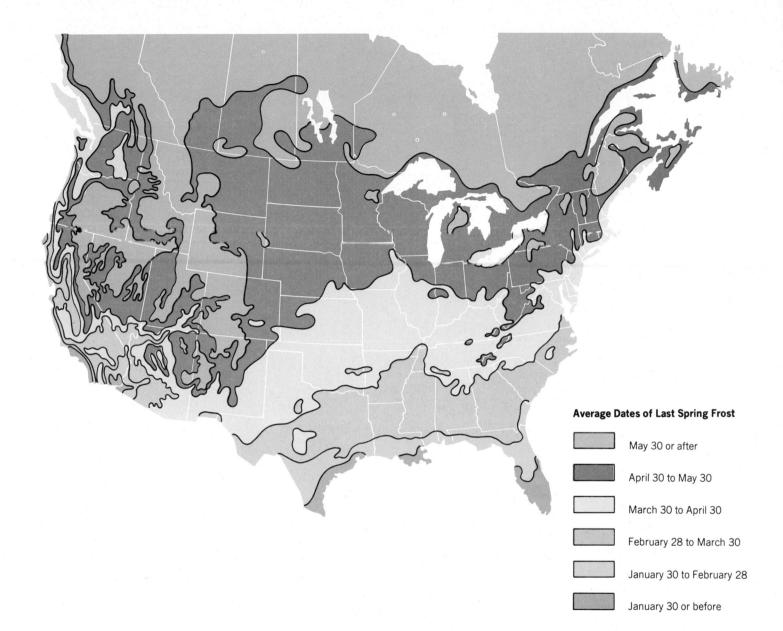

Average Dates of Last Spring Frost

May 30 or after

April 30 to May 30

March 30 to April 30

February 28 to March 30

January 30 to February 28

January 30 or before

Patterns of warmth and cold. This map, which depicts the average dates of the last spring frosts, is valuable in landscaping, although no charts in the book refer directly to it. The map divides the United States and Canada into six final-frost zones; its legend keys the colors of the zones to dates. Use the map to gauge the approximate time, in your area, of the transition from late winter to early spring; this is a critical period in seasonal yard work. The Check List of Seasonal Chores (*pages 124-125*) is based in part on the assumption that such tasks as fertilizing, renewing mulch and transplanting will be performed after the last killing cold. The map has its limitations. In any locality, the end of a winter may vary from the norm by as much as two weeks; what is more, depending on location, your house and yard may be subject to climatic idiosyncracies produced by elevation, local wind patterns, exposure to the sun, or proximity to a body of water. For information about conditions in your specific locality, consult the nearest office of the U.S. Weather Bureau, an agricultural extension service or a local nursery.

A Check List of Seasonal Chores

A landscaped yard requires year-round care to stay healthy and beautiful, and each season calls for its own set of chores. Spring is a time of planting and of preparing for the coming season of heavy growth. In summer, the homeowner must maintain fast-growing lawns and gardens with watering, weeding, trimming and cutting. Fall chores consist mainly of preparation for winter but usually include some planting as well. And winter in cold climates means taking steps to protect plants from ice and snow, and planning for the coming spring.

Because of the wide variations in climate in North America, you cannot rely solely on the calendar to mark the divisions between seasons. For the most part, use changes in temperature, weather and soil conditions as a guide.

Changes in temperature and in the relative lengths of day and night are obvious clues. Spring comes after the danger of hard frost has passed, when bulbs begin to put out shoots, and perennial plants unfurl new leaves and stems. Summer is the heart of the growing season—the time of the highest temperatures and the longest days of the year. Fall approaches as days shorten and temperatures drop; in all of Canada and most of the United States, the season has arrived when the nighttime temperature dips regularly to 55° F. or below. Late fall is the time after the first few killing frosts, and winter—the period when most plants are dormant—has the shortest days and lowest temperatures of the year.

Changes in soil and growing conditions are more subtle. If you are unsure of the clues that mark the seasons in your locality, ask your agricultural extension agent or experienced gardeners.

In the check list that follows, the essential chores for each season are named in a brief list. More information about these tasks is given in the paragraphs below. To find detailed instructions for each job, refer to the index and the preceding pages of this book.

Early Spring

REMOVE WINTER COVERINGS
CLEAN UP WINTER DEBRIS
RENEW MULCH
FEED GROUND COVERS
SPRAY DORMANT TREES

When the last heavy snows of winter have melted away, remove burlap or other protective coverings from shrubs and plants. Any late snows will probably not be heavy enough to damage branches. Pull old mulch away from the shrub stems, and rake leaves and other debris off the lawn and ground covers.

After this cleanup, mix the old mulch into the soil and lay new mulch around shrubs. Fertilize ground covers; run hedge clippers or a lawn mower at its highest cutting level over ground-cover beds to eliminate stringy top growth.

Before many leaf buds open, spray trees and shrubs with a dormant-oil spray or an all-purpose spray for pest control. Early spring is also the time to begin a general pruning of shrubs and trees and to do the hard spring pruning of roses.

If you plowed up a vegetable garden in the fall to condition the soil, use a bow rake to smooth the soil for replanting. In the flower garden, plant new perennials and fertilize old ones. Reseed bare spots in the lawn, then spread slow-acting lime and fertilizer over the entire expanse of grass and water it.

Midspring

CUT GRASS
TRANSPLANT SHRUBS AND TREES
PULL WEEDS

Midspring marks the start of the repetitive maintenance tasks that your plants will need throughout the growing season. A first cutting of the grass is needed; a regimen of crab-grass control should be started, and a preemergent weed killer should be applied to the lawn.

In both the lawn and gardens, weeding should begin on a weekly basis. Begin edging the plant beds, and tie up the leaves of bulbs that completed their flowering in early spring; alternatively, six to eight weeks after flowering, dig up the bulbs for storage until the fall.

When the soil is dry enough to work easily, you can plant or transplant most trees and shrubs, both deciduous and evergreen. (A second opportunity for planting trees and shrubs will come in the fall.) Midspring is also the time to begin planting a vegetable garden.

Late Spring

PLANT ANNUALS
PRUNE SHRUBS

Plant any remaining perennials and all of your annuals, along with tender bulbs such as cannas and dahlias. Begin spring pruning of shrubs that do not flower or that will flower in late summer or fall. (Wait until spring-blooming shrubs have lost their blossoms before pruning them.) Check the lawn periodically to see if the soil needs more or less water than your regular watering program is providing.

Early Summer

PERFORM GENERAL SPRAYING
PRUNE HEDGES
EDGE AND WEED

As spring gives way to summer, apply pesticides to control fungus, insects, disease and scale on all plants that are especially susceptible to these afflictions. For the best results with roses, continue spraying or dusting them once a week until the end of the growing season.

Shape hedges and borders, and remove faded blossoms from annuals to stimulate further bloom. If you have a pond, this is a good time to plant delicate water flowers, such as waterlilies and lotuses.

Midsummer

WATER
WEED
CUT GRASS LONGER

As the summer proceeds, a combination of strong sun, periods of drought and drying winds creates a danger of leaf scorch. Keep all plants watered well to prevent damage; take special care to give any trees and shrubs that were planted in the spring a periodic soaking. Weed flower and shrub beds, and continue to remove faded blossoms from annuals and perennials. Divide any perennials that have finished blooming, discarding the dead centers; replant the good shoots.

To protect a lawn from summer heat, start cutting the grass about 1 inch longer than you did in spring, so that it will not burn out. Test the soil of the lawn to determine the conditioning that it will require in the fall.

Late Summer

SOW GRASS SEED
FERTILIZE LAWN
PERFORM SPRAYING IF NEEDED
ORDER BULBS

The shorter days and cooler nights of late summer signal the time to start new lawns or renovate old ones. This is also a time to watch for increases in any pest population severe enough to warrant a second application of pesticide. Examine your plants for possible iron deficiency caused by their summer growth spurt: If you see yellow leaves with dark green veins, feed the plants with an iron-rich fertilizer; check the soil pH and drainage.

Continue regular weeding and watering. Take care not to overwater; moderating temperatures begin reducing the plants' moisture requirements.

Begin watching the advertisements of local garden-supply stores. You can buy and plant fall-flowering bulbs as soon as they come on the market in your area. Order spring-flowering bulbs.

Early Fall

FINISH LAWN RENOVATION
TRANSPLANT TREES AND SHRUBS
PLANT BULBS
START COMPOST PILE

Aerate the lawn, and dethatch it if necessary. Continue to mow the lawn regularly as long as the grass keeps growing, although you can cut it shorter and less often once summer's heat has broken; apply lime if needed.

Fall is a good time to dig up and move evergreen shrubs and trees or to plant new ones. Wait until after the leaves of deciduous plants fall before moving them. Bare-rooted roses can be planted, as can spring-flowering bulbs. Be sure to water new plants regularly and mulch them lightly to help control weeds.

If you do not have a compost pile, fall is an excellent time to start one; your general prewinter cleanup will soon produce a steady supply of compostable vegetable tops, dead or dying annuals, fallen leaves and other items.

Deep-feed the roots of trees, especially ornamental ones, and dig up tender tuberous bulbs, such as gladiolus, for storage in a frost-free place over the winter.

Late Fall

RAKE LEAVES
PRUNE ROSES
CUT PERENNIALS
CHECK MULCH
BRING IN EQUIPMENT

Late fall is the time for a last flurry of activity before winter. Leaves must be cleared from lawns and ground covers. Older needles shedding off pine trees must be raked up. (They make a good mulch for shrubs.)

The last pruning of roses should be completed in time to prepare the plants for winter; cut off long stems, so that they cannot be whipped by winter winds. Cut down herbaceous, or fleshy, perennials, and cover the stubble with mulch or evergreen boughs. Prune trees and hedges one last time before winter. Dig up annuals after the first killing frost.

Mulch should be renewed or repaired on all shrubs at this time. Use a pronged cultivator to stir up mulch that has become so compacted that air and water cannot get to the plants.

Scrape dirt, rust and grass off the lawn mower, remove the spark plug and drain out the oil and gasoline. Then replace the oil and store the mower. Empty, clean and store your sprayers and dusters.

Dig dead plants out of the vegetable garden and add them to the compost pile. Spread manure or rough compost. Turn over the soil with a spade or a tiller, leaving it in large clods.

Until freezing temperatures set in, water all plants well one morning a week to give them the moisture they need to weather the winter. Close any irrigation systems, turn off outside spigots and bring in hoses and tools for storage.

Early Winter

PROTECT SHRUBS
PRUNE EVERGREENS
REMOVE DEAD LEAVES
REPAIR TOOLS

If severe winter storms are common in your area, be sure to protect shrubs and delicate trees from the coming ravages of ice, snow and wind. Use evergreen clippings, such as those from a Christmas tree, to cover low shrubs; wrap medium-sized ones with burlap. Build a roofed shelter around the plants under the eaves of your house, to shield the branches from snow sliding off the roof. Protect broad-leaved evergreens from transpiration—the evaporation of water through leaves—with antitranspirant spray.

Trim hollies and other broad-leaved evergreens for indoor decorations; the pruning will improve the health of the plants as well. Rake leaves from lawns and perennial beds; matted leaves can choke lawn grasses and promote disease.

Check your garden tools at this point in the year to see if they need to be sharpened, repaired or replaced. Test soil from gardens and shrub beds so that the results will be on hand in time for spring soil conditioning and planting.

Midwinter

KEEP PLANTS FREE OF SNOW
PRUNE ORNAMENTAL TREES
ORDER SEEDS, SHRUBS, PERENNIALS

During the dead of winter, the major chore is still that of protecting plants from the elements. Check and repair protective coverings frequently and, after each snowstorm, gently shake or broom the snow from branches. Apply a second coating of antitranspirant to broad-leaved evergreens. When clearing walks and driveways, take care not to shovel snow onto bordering plants. Instead of using plant killing salts to melt snow near lawns and gardens, use fertilizer or wood ashes.

After bad storms, cut broken branches from shrubs and trees. On mild days, finish pruning trees and shrubs that flowered in the late summer and fall. Order seeds, shrubs and perennials from mail-order catalogues for spring planting.

Picture Credits

The sources for the illustrations in this book are listed below. The drawings were created by Jack Arthur, Roger Essley, William J. Hennessy Jr., John Jones, Dick Lee and Joan McGurren.

Cover: Fil Hunter. 6-11: Fil Hunter. 12-15: Graham Sayles. 17-21: Eduino J. Pereira. 23-25: John Massey. 26, 27: William J. Hennessy Jr. from A and W Graphics. 29-31: Stephen Turner. 33-35: William J. Hennessy Jr. from A and W Graphics. 36: Fil Hunter. 39-47: Walter Hilmers Studios. 48-53: Arezou Katoozian from A and W Graphics. 56-60: Adisai Hemintranont· from Sai Graphis. 64: Fil Hunter. 67-74: Jennifer and John Massey. 75-80: Adisai Hemintranont from Sai Graphis. 85-93: Frederic F. Bigio from B-C Graphics. 96, 97: Frederic F. Bigio from B-C Graphics. 98: Fil Hunter. 101-109: Frederic F. Bigio from B-C Graphics. 110-114: Elsie J. Hennig. 116-121: Elsie J. Hennig.

Acknowledgments

The index/glossary for this book was prepared by Louise Hedberg. The editors also thank: Joan S. Banfield, Rockville, Md.; Cheryl Bledins, Little Giant Pump Co., Oklahoma City, Okla.; Brookside Gardens, Maryland National Capital Park and Planning Commission, Wheaton, Md.; Jim Campbell, Campbell & Ferrara Nurseries, Inc., Alexandria, Va.; Larry Enten, Enten's Landscaping, Washington, D.C.; Keith Folsom, Lilypons Water Gardens, Lilypons, Md.; Gaines Hardware, Alexandria, Va.; Robert M. Jones, Alexandria, Va.; Lynn Makela, Springfield, Va.; Bernie Nees, Burtonsville, Md.; Erik Neumann, Curator of Education, Mary Ann Jarvis, Program Assistant, Education Department, U.S. National Arboretum, Washington. D.C.; Franziska Reed-Hecht, Gardening for Everyone, Washington, D.C.; Don Smith, Superintendent of Gardens and Grounds, Dumbarton Oaks, Washington, D.C.; Ralph H. Smith, Washington, D.C.

Index/Glossary

Included in this index are definitions of many of the technical terms used in this book. Page references in italics indicate an illustration of the subject mentioned.

Aerator, loosening compacted soil, *11, 38, 45*

Annuals: flowers, planting, 97; vines, *chart* 63

Aquatic plants, cultivating, *104*

Arbor: building, *118-119*; posts for, 116, *118*

Archway, *119-121*; arch templates, *120*; support posts, 116, *119*

Baffles: *steplike obstructions set into a hillside.* Erecting, 26

Berms and swales: *ridges and depressions constructed on a slope, for the purpose of redirecting water flow*; 26, 27

Biennials, 96

Branch collar: *enlarged area at the base of a branch.* Importance to pruning, 66, 67, 68, 69

Bulbs: buying, 96; planting, 97

Check list of seasonal chores, 124-125

Climate: frost dates, *map* 123; zones of, *map* 122. *See also* Growing areas

Compost: adding to heap, *35*; enriching soil, 32

Cuttings, taking of: *method of propagation.* For ground covers, *58-59*; for shrubs, 90

Deciduous plants: ground covers, 56, *chart* 61; trees, 66, *chart* 82-83; vines, *chart* 63

Design, principles of, to use in landscaping, *18-21*

Dethatching: *removing layer of dead grass that clogs fresh growth in a lawn*; 38, 46

Dividing: *method of propagation.* For ground covers, 58, 59

Dormant oil: *emulsion of mineral oil and water.* Spraying on trees, 66

Double digging: *technique of preparing soil*; 32, 34

Drainage, 22, 26; berms and swales, 26, 27; building a retaining wall, 28, *29-31*; erecting baffles, 26; terracing a slope, 26, 27; testing soil for, 26

Espalier, trellis for, *118*

Evergreens: ground covers, 56, *chart* 61; shrubs, *chart* 95; trees, 66, *chart* 83; vines, *chart* 63

Fertilizer: applying with trough spreader, *44*; broadcasting on lawn, *44*; composition of, 38; for established lawn, 38, *44*; for shrubs, 84; for trees, 66, *70-71*; use during the year, 124-125; for vines, 62

Flowers: caring for perennials, 97; planning a bed for continuous bloom, 96; planting bulbs, 97

Fountains: connecting to pool, *104*; pump for, 100, *104*

Frost, dates of average last spring, *map* 123

Garden structures: fountain, *104*; pool, 100, *101-104*; rock garden, *111-115*; supports for vines, *116-121*; waterfall, *105-110*

Grading: digging and moving earth, 22, 23; leveling site, 24; setting slope, 25

Grasses: to choose when planting new lawn, 50; climatic zones, *map* 55; cool-season, 50; fertilizing, 38, *44*; mowing, 38, *39, 40-41*; seeding new lawn, *50-53*; and soil acidity, 38; varieties of, *chart* 54; warm-season, 50. *See also* Lawn care

Ground covers: buying flats, 56; cuttings, *58-59*; deciduous, 56, *chart* 61; dividing, 58, 59; evergreen, 56, *chart* 61; growing on a slope, 60; herbaceous, 56, *chart* 61; layering, 58; planting, 56, *57*; semi-evergreen, *chart* 61; in a stone wall, 60; varieties and growing requirements of, *chart* 61; weeding, 56. *See also* Vines

Growing areas: climatic zones, *map* 122; evergreen shrubs, *chart* 95, *map* 81; flowering shrubs, *chart* 94-95; grasses, *chart* 54, *map* 55; ground covers, *chart* 61; rock-garden plants, *chart* 115; trees, *chart* 82-83, *map* 81; vines, *chart* 63

Hedge, trimming, *87*

Hose, garden: repairing leak with kit, 12, *13*; replacing coupling of, 12, *13*; storing, 12

Insecticides, and trees, 66, *72. See also* Pest control; Spraying

Lawn: direct seeding, 50, *51*; establishing a new, *50-53*; laying sod, 50, *53*; planting with sprigs or plugs, 50, *52-53*; putting down artificial turf, 47; rolling, *50*; selecting grasses based on soil and climate, 50, *chart* 54, *map* 55

Lawn care, 37; compacted soil, *45*; during the year, 124-125; edging, *41*; fertilizing, 38, *44*; mowing, 38, *39, 40-41*; removing thatch, 38, *46*; reseeding bare spots, 38, *47*; watering, 38, *42-43*; weeding, *48-49*

Layering: *method of propagation.* For ground covers, 58; for shrubs, 90, *93*

Logs, clearing site of, *24*

Lime, for reducing acidity in soil, 32

Mattock, *10*; replacing handle, *15*

Mowing: during the year, 124-125; edging, *41*; mowers, *39*; mowing strip, 38; recommended heights to cut grass, 38, *54*; safety and, 38; setting blade height, *40*

Mowing strip: *concrete or brick border at edge of a lawn*; 38

Mulching: during the year, 124-125; ground covers, 56; perennials, 97; shrubs, 84, *86*; vines, 62

Perennials: dividing, 97; grown from seed, 97; vines, *chart* 63; winter care, 97

Pergola: *series of archways built over a path.* Constructing, 116, *121*

Pest control: biological, 66; by dormant oil sprayed on trees, 66; and trees, 66, *72*; and vines, 62

Planning a yard, 7, 16, *17-21*; mapping existing yard, 16, *17*; principles of design, *18-21*; selecting appropriate plantings, 16

Plot plan: *map that defines size and shape of property*; 16, *17*

Pool, fiberglass garden: aquatic plants growing in, *104*; calculating pump size, 100; circulating water in, 100; connecting pump to electrical circuit, 100, *101, 102-103*; excavating and filling, *101*; using pump to power a fountain, 100, *104*

Preemergent weed killer, 48

Propagation, methods of: by cuttings, *58-59, 90*; by dividing, 58, *59*; by layering, 58, 90, *93*

Pruning: during the year, 124-125; of large branches, *68*; of newly planted trees, 75, *79*; painting the wound, 66; of roses, *88*; of shrubs, 84, *86-88*; timing of, 66; tools for, *68-69*; of trees, 66, *67-69*

Pump: circulating water in a pool, 100, *101*; electrical hookups, 100, *101, 102-*